From Iron Lung to Iron Butt

Riding Polio Into History

Lynda Lahman

Cover photo courtesy of Tom Paniagua

ISBN-10: 1499300107
ISBN-13: 978-1499300109

FOREWORD

Tragic incidences of polio can be traced back centuries through drawings and writings of ancient scribes. The poliovirus — poliomyelitis — is often referred to as "infantile paralysis" as it has caused lifelong crippling effects and death to millions of our most vulnerable and helpless victims... the children.

Much has been written on the challenges to overcome the disease and the dramatic search for an effective immunization against poliovirus. Bob Mutchler's story provides a personal account of the impact of the disease upon an infant and his parents, as well as the ensuing experiences of an adult living and coping with the continuing ravages of polio.

Bob Mutchler had the rare opportunity to become a member of a Rotary club in the earliest days of Rotary International's commitment to eradicate polio. In the early 1980s, when the disease was paralyzing or killing 1000 youngsters per day, the worldwide organization of Rotary initiated a program called PolioPlus to provide immunizations to children around the globe.

In his unique way, Bob rallied his energy and determination to make his own contribution to Rotary's cause of universal polio immunization. This is the gripping story of a boy who knew from his own experiences exactly what a "world without polio" could

mean to children and families who would no longer fear
the nightmare of poliomyelitis.

An innovative spokesman, "Motorcycle Bob" has effectively raised
national and international awareness of the urgency to
immunize all children against polio.

~ Cliff Dochterman, President, Rotary International, 1992-93

PROLOGUE

My first memory of polio is lining up in the school auditorium, anxiously waiting my turn for the dreaded shot in my arm. A few years later I remember being given the Sabin oral vaccine, and while not really understanding what it was for, I enjoyed sucking on a cube of sugar with my mother's full approval.

Other than making sure my own children were vaccinated, the disease faded from my awareness; a tale from long ago and far away. That was true until I met Bob. Hearing his story made the impact of the disease real for me.

Having read my book about motorcycling, he asked me for a small favor. "I can give speeches about polio, but I can't write to save my life. I need you to put my story on paper," he implored. "It's an important journey about a war that has yet to be won."

The story that follows is his, channeled through me.
The fight belongs to all of us.

~ Lynda Lahman

CHAPTER 1

I have seen the photograph of my father proudly introducing me to his motorcycle, though his first attempt at giving me a ride on it was thwarted by the nurses at the hospital. They didn't approve of a one-day-old baby being transported home in a mother's arms on the back seat of a two-wheeled motorized machine. I had to wait until my third day for that experience.

Pushing limits was nothing new for my father, nor was riding motorcycles. Growing up in Bloomsburg, Pennsylvania, he was riding almost as soon as he could walk. He tried to impress my mother by racing up and down the street in front of the small store where she worked. She thought he was an uncouth show-off, filled with a big head and a foul mouth. But he was very determined and kept bothering her. Hoping to get him to leave her alone, she agreed to go out with him, but only if he picked her up in a car and watched his language.

Apparently that did the trick, and they were soon married. At first, my father worked as a piano tuner alongside his father, but he felt stifled in Bloomsburg. So, looking to expand his employment opportunities, my parents, with their baby daughter Ginnie, moved to Brownsville, Texas, a spot chosen randomly for its promise of warmth and sunshine. Freed from the watchful eyes of her family, my mother proved to be less prim than she pretended to be, and was soon riding all over town on her own Harley, having no interest in simply being a passenger.

My father, strong-willed and stubborn, had a bad temper, normally limited to yelling. One night, during a heated argument, he lost control and shoved my mother into a wall. Believing she had made a terrible mistake, she filed for divorce, a bold move for a woman in 1945. She took Ginnie and returned to her parents in Bloomsburg. Writing letters back and forth, my mother's fears began to dissipate, and it was clear my parents still loved each other. Soon my mother, hoping my father had changed from this experience, returned to Texas where they remarried.

Nine months later my sister, Dixie, was born, but when she was barely eighteen-months-old, tragedy struck. Happy and healthy when my mother put her to bed one night, she was unresponsive the following morning. Her normally warm, cuddly body was cold and stiff. Shaking her, screaming for my father, desperately trying everything she could, my mother couldn't bring Dixie's tiny heart back to life. Their beautify baby girl was dead. SIDS — Sudden Infant Death Syndrome. Consumed with grief, they closed up emotionally, refusing to share even the barest details of her brief life with anyone.

Pregnant shortly after losing Dixie, my mother kept her anxiety to herself. My parents were relieved when I arrived July 15, 1947, a healthy and robust baby boy whom they christened Robert after my father.

My mother kept her fears pushed aside during the day, only to have them overwhelm her each night after putting us to bed. She snuck into my room to check on me as I slept, images of Dixie never far from her mind, and relaxed slightly each time I reached another milestone. Rolling over, sitting up by myself, reaching for toys brought moments of pleasure and helped alleviate the nightmares that continued to torture her sleep. Listening to me as I giggled and bounced in my playpen, covered with fine netting to keep the incessant bugs off my delicate skin, she felt herself beginning to enjoy motherhood once again. Together, my parents celebrated when I took my first tentative steps, grabbing onto tables and chairs until I felt bold enough to let go and try it on my own.

My mother cherished our bedtime rituals: while Ginnie, almost four, ate a small snack and I drank my last bottle of the day, she read us one of my sister's favorite bedtime stories, rocking me gently until I nodded off to sleep. Then she'd place me in my crib in the room I shared with my sister, turn on the small nightlight in the corner, and blow Ginnie a kiss. Leaving our door slightly ajar, she quietly retreated to the living room to read until she could no longer keep her eyes open, once again hoping her exhaustion might spare her from her recurring dreams.

And every morning my mother tiptoed toward our room, silently catching us as we chatted unawares. She quietly peeked through the door and watched for a few moments as Ginnie, always very serious, pretended to read to me from her favorite picture book, turning it now and then to show me the illustrations just like she'd seen the librarian do, and I hung onto the bars of my crib, gurgling and laughing.

My parents loved the springtime in south Texas. The sunshine brought warmth and the chance to be outside, and April 1948 was no exception. Winter blankets were already stored, my sister and I needing only light sleepers at night. As was her habit, my mother came toward our room early one morning and was surprised to hear only silence. Assuming I was still asleep, she tiptoed up to my crib.

Why is Bobby still lying down? He's usually the first one awake, she thought as she walked across the room. She looked into the crib and froze. I was wide awake, flat on my back, my legs at an odd angle to my body.

"Bobby! What's wrong with your legs?" She reached in to pick me up. I screamed.

"Bob! The baby's not moving right! He's screaming uncontrollably; I can't get him to stop crying!" she called out to my father in the other room. My wailing increased, my arms flailing as my legs hung motionless.

"It's okay, sweetie, it's okay; Mommy's here." Her attempts to soothe me only incited more shrieks. Ginnie, terrified by the fear in my mother's voice, huddled on her bed, clutching her teddy bear.

"What's wrong, Mama?" she whimpered, beginning to cry.

"Bob, we need to get him to the doctor immediately! Something is horribly wrong," my mother yelled as my father ran into the room, her own voice catching as she held back her sobs.

"I'll take Ginnie to the neighbor's and get the car. Grab the diaper bag. I'll meet you outside," my father instructed, hoping to give them both something to focus on besides their panic. Scooping up Ginnie, he hustled down the hallway while my mother concentrated on gathering the bag from the floor and I wailed in her arms.

"Faster, Bob; can't you go any faster!" My mother's voice inched toward panic. The short drive to the doctor's felt like a lifetime. Her touch, rather than soothing me, elicited piercing screams. "I can't make him stop! I don't know what's happening!"

"Help us! Something is dreadfully wrong with our baby!" my father blurted out as they burst into the empty waiting room, the doctor's office having just opened for the day. The nurse took us into an examining room, her calm demeanor in stark contrast to my parents' anxiety.

"Well, I know this looks very scary, but I've seen this before. You really have nothing to worry about," the doctor's soft voice and soothing words reassured my mother as he quietly explained his diagnosis. "Kids sometimes get vitamin deficiencies, causing painful cramps in their legs. I'm 100 percent sure that's what we're seeing here. We'll get him on a regime of vitamins and minerals and he'll be better in no time."

"Are you sure? It came on so suddenly; we were petrified. We were worried it was something much worse," the relief evident in my mother's voice as she discreetly dabbed at the tears in her eyes. Quickly picking me up to regain her composure, she turned again to the doctor. "We'll start him on the vitamins right away. Thank you so much for your help."

They closely monitored every bite I ate, mashing the supplements into tiny spoonfuls of applesauce to slip unnoticed down my throat. My mother hovered over me, looking for the slightest signs of improvement, knowing it might be weeks before I benefited from the treatments. Listening to my cries whenever she touched or moved my legs was as torturous for her as the pain was for me. She desperately wanted to believe I would be well soon, her bouncy baby boy once again.

Two weeks passed without any progress. No longer able to sit upright unattended, my legs still flopped erratically whenever anyone picked me up. My mother, who had already begun having doubts, was now seriously questioning the doctor's diagnosis and competence. She felt helpless to solve this mysterious affliction that had occurred literally overnight.

"Mom, I can't do this much longer. I'm exhausted and Bobby isn't getting better." Despite the poor phone connection, my grandmother could hear the desperation in my mother's voice. "I need help."

"I'll be on the next train down," my grandmother reassured her. She arrived within days, bringing with her renewed hope along with news of a treatment she had heard might ease my pain.

Offering to sacrifice her favorite woolen blanket, my grandmother tore it into strips and soaked the pieces in boiling water. Once the strips cooled just enough to keep them from burning my fragile skin, she wrapped them around my tiny limbs. It was the only thing either of them could do to stop my crying.

Nothing helped. Normally extremely private, in a fit of frustration, my mother shared her concerns with a friend, who in turn, passed them on to her husband — a dentist.

"This isn't normal. You need to have someone else see him immediately, and don't take no for an answer. Demand every test imaginable, including a spinal tap," the friend insisted, relaying the information her husband had shared with her. "We're both quite concerned that you get the right help."

My grandmother suggested they return to Pennsylvania, believing there were better medical facilities than in rural Texas. Packing my sister and me in the car, my parents drove over 2,000 miles to Bloomsburg. They left Ginnie with my grandparents and drove another 200 miles to Pittsburgh to have me evaluated at Children's Hospital. I cried most of the way.

Racing through the front doors of the hospital, my parents were greeted by a nurse who, upon seeing my flaccid legs, immediately steered them into a small examination room.

"Wait here. Don't leave the room for any reason. The doctor will be in momentarily." Surprised at the urgency in her voice, they obeyed. My father paced the small space, pretending to look at the posters on the walls while my mother rocked me gently. Neither one spoke.

The quiet knock startled them both. Pushing open the door, the young physician held out his hand to greet my father. Then after washing his hands, he turned to my mother, inviting her to lay me down on the cold metal table.

"Let's check this young fellow out, why don't we? He doesn't look too happy today," the doctor's cheerful tone masked the seriousness of his demeanor as he began a thorough examination, checking me from head to toe. "I'd like to take some blood to see what we find, and I'd also like to get a sample of his spinal fluid. I'll need you to leave when I do that. You can step outside to wait and I'll let you know when we're finished." Calling for the nurse, he pointed to a row of chairs for us to sit on. "It won't take long."

He soon came back out. "We'll let you know what we find as soon as we get the results. I'd like you to leave Bobby here with the nurses while you wait in the lobby."

Unsure what else to do, my parents followed his directions, and sat for what seemed like an eternity. A receptionist finally motioned them to follow her into an office. The doctor came in shortly, his grave expression confirming their worst fears. Whatever it was, it was serious.

"The physician in Brownsville made a terrible mistake. I have no idea what led him to believe this was a vitamin deficiency. Your son's symptoms are very distinctive. The paralysis and the sensitivity to touch are the classic trademarks of polio. I noticed him also having struggles with his breathing. The spinal tap confirmed our suspicions."

Grabbing my father's arm for support, my mother held her breath and tears filled her eyes. No one said a word as the doctor's words sank in. All my mother knew about polio was that it was a killer. Were they about to lose another baby? How could she bear this? She wanted to make him stop, make his words disappear, make it all go away.

The doctor continued, his voice almost cold as he rattled off facts and figures. My parents heard only snippets of the conversation, terrified of what he might say next.

"As you know, there is no cure. It may get worse.

"This disease is unpredictable. I think it's also in his chest, and it's possible he may need to be placed in an iron lung if his breathing deteriorates further.

"If it progresses too far or too fast, he may die.

"It's also possible he may recover completely. We can only treat his symptoms, and pray."

Struggling to comprehend, helpless to do or say anything, my parents wanted to do what was right. Their only hope was to listen to the doctor, to trust in him to save my life. His words kept coming at them.

"He needs to be put into quarantine immediately. You need to leave him here, right now, today.

"You can see him very briefly to say goodbye, but then I'm going to insist you stay away from him until we are sure he is no longer contagious. I honestly have no idea when that will be."

Stunned, the doctor led them back to the tiny examining room. The nurse moved away from my bedside and turned her back, giving my parents a moment of privacy. Sobbing, my mother reached for me and picked me up, cradling me in her arms.

Humming her favorite lullaby, she gently rocked side to side. "You'll be okay, sweetie. The kind doctors and nurses will take care of you and make you all better. We'll come back as soon as we can. We'll be thinking of you constantly. It's going to be okay."

The words, spoken in a whisper only I could hear, were as much for her reassurance as they were for me. My father, normally stoic and strong, wept silently in the corner, barely believing what was happening.

"I'm sorry, but you need to leave now," the nurse spoke softly into my mother's ear. "We have to put him in the isolation ward. I promise we'll take good care of him."

Placing me in the nurse's arms, her heaving sobs wracking her chest, my mother patted my head one last time and turned away. Grabbing the doorframe, she looked back one final time. My father put his arms around her and gently pulled her away.

"We have to do this. It's our only chance to get our baby boy back. We have to trust this is the right thing to do." He was convincing himself as much as he was convincing her. Neither one really knew what would happen next.

~

Spring turned to summer, and soon drifted into fall. Christmas came and went, which I spent in the hospital, surrounded by other patients, nurses, and staff. Eight months passed before my parents were allowed to return for their first visit, and by then they had become strangers to me.

I entered the hospital in 1948 and wasn't discharged until June 1951, three long years after my parents watched me taken down that hallway, and just weeks before my fourth birthday. Like most children, I don't have many memories of my earliest years. Unlike most children, my parents are unable to fill in the blanks with photos or stories from their own recollections.

They weren't there to capture them.

1947

Dr. Jonas Salk begins work at the University of Pittsburgh School of Medicine. A year later he begins research toward developing a vaccine against polio.

CHAPTER 2

In 1948, America's fear of the atomic bomb was surpassed only by its fear of polio. Happy and playing one day, paralyzed from the neck down the next, no one knew what caused it or how it spread. Because only a very small percentage of victims showed outward signs of the disease, the virus moved unnoticed until a case of paralysis revealed the otherwise invisible monster. Paralytic polio sometimes descended upon a single family, striking one child and leaving the others spared, or causing the deaths of several siblings within weeks. Entire towns were affected while neighboring towns were left untouched.

Anxiety and rumor were rampant, resulting in quarantines, isolation, and avoidance of anyone even suspected of being connected in any way to the disease, yet nothing seemed to help prevent the spread of the virus. Once a case appeared in a town, parents kept their kids inside, believing they could protect them within the walls of their own homes. Restaurants stood empty, streets were quiet, and movie theaters were abandoned. Schools frequently burned books, fearing invisible germs might spread to other innocent victims. Public health workers launched programs that immediately removed anyone from their families who showed signs of the disease, placing them in isolation without even a chance to say goodbye. Incidents spiked in summertime, with groups of children playing together outside enjoying warmer temperatures.

Evidence of polio exists throughout history. Ancient drawings depict sufferers with withered limbs and leaning on canes, and stories are told of a Roman emperor who walked with a limp. Major epidemics, however, did not make their appearance until the twentieth century, when they began occurring with increasing frequency in the United States and Europe. In addition, prior to the 1900s most cases of polio affected children between the ages of six months and four years. As the incidences of epidemics spread, so did the age of the average victim. Scientists, public health officials, and researchers were challenged to solve this mysterious new puzzle.

Early theories assumed polio was transmitted through the respiratory system, entering the nose and migrating to the brain. Discovering that the virus entered the mouth through water contaminated by feces, passing hand-to-hand, in food, or while playing in dirty water, led to new approaches for prevention. Efforts to contain the disease focused on areas public health workers were familiar with — poor hygiene, lack of decent sanitation, poverty, pollution, and airborne carriers, such as flies. However, it was soon apparent that the larger outbreaks were occurring in middle class suburbs rather than slums. Outlying areas, rather than inner cities, were hardest hit.

Constant low level exposure to any virus often leads to a natural immunity which can be passed, temporarily, from mother to child either in utero or through breastfeeding. As the child is exposed to viruses gradually in the environment, and the protections from the mother fade, the child's immune system begins to develop its own resistance.

As hygiene improved, at first among the higher, more affluent classes who could afford indoor plumbing, and then to other areas as overall sanitation systems improved, children were no longer naturally exposed to small doses of the virus. Unable to develop their own immunity, they became easy targets as they outgrew the protections supplied from their mothers at birth. The once rare disease turned into a killer.

Polio occurs in three forms. Type I, or spinal polio, involves the trunk of the body and the legs, and is the most common. Damaged by inflammation, nerve cells die and the muscles they control weaken and atrophy, becoming paralyzed within two to four days. Impairment is often asymmetrical, attacking one side of the body or one limb more than the other. Type II, or bulbar polio, affects the portion of the brain that controls the nerves used for speaking, swallowing, moving the upper neck, as well as breath rate, rhythm, and depth. Death can result from suffocation or respiratory arrest. Type III, bulbospinal or respiratory polio, affects the spinal cord and can cause paralysis of the diaphragm, often making it impossible to breathe unassisted. In addition, it can paralyze limbs and affect swallowing and the functioning of the heart.

Most epidemics, particularly in the US, stem from Type I. Entering the body through the mouth, the virus moves quickly to the gastrointestinal tract where it rapidly multiplies. Most of those who get the virus will show no symptoms, but for approximately one percent of its victims, the virus will continue on a relentless attack, entering the bloodstream where it is carried to the central nervous system. There it destroys motor neuron cells, which control the muscles used for movement, swallowing, breathing, and circulation. Before the invention of the respirator, patients were placed in an iron lung, a mechanical breathing apparatus that utilizes air pressure to expand and contract the chest. The enormous machines encased almost the entire body, forcing patients to lie on their backs in a giant tube with only their heads sticking out. Even then, deaths occurred with regularity.

Prior to the 1940s the general medical consensus was to keep the affected limbs straight and immobilized in rigid braces and full body casts while the virus ran its course. Instead, the treatments designed to help actually contributed to greater muscle atrophy. Beginning in 1928, an Australian woman, Sister Kenny, practiced an unconventional and controversial method, believing continual movement combined with hot compresses would prevent atrophy in the limbs and would recall function in non-affected neural pathways. Sister Kenny, a non-credentialed self-taught nurse, created an uproar as she promoted her methods worldwide. Often derided by those in the medical establishment, she received substantial support in the US, teaching her approach to receptive physicians.

I was one of the lucky ones who benefited from Sister Kenny's dedication to helping those with polio. I believe whatever function I have today is because of the efforts of the nurses, my grandmother, and my mother who continually stimulated my legs with heat packs, massage, and movement. Other, less effective but extremely painful treatments I — and countless others — endured, were experimental surgeries severing tightened tendons and transplanting muscles in vain attempts to restore function to damaged legs.

Patients were placed in wards filled with others suffering a wide degree of symptoms. Iron lungs lined walls, the 'whoosh, whoosh' of the air a constant background hum. Patients screamed, often for hours on end; polio is an extremely painful disease. Babies in cribs cried for their mothers, older children told stories to each other as they laid in their beds unable to move, and families visited when they were allowed to come or were able to make the journey depending on the distances they needed to travel. Some children, abandoned by families ashamed of the stigma of polio or unable to care for the severity of their paralysis, had no hopes of leaving. Nurses and therapists were constantly present, monitoring breathing and performing the stretching exercises that would help restore functioning to otherwise motionless limbs. During epidemics, the wards were filled beyond capacity, with rows and rows of beds encroaching on space otherwise devoted to treating other illnesses.

In 1921, an athletic, otherwise healthy, thirty-eight-year-old aspiring politician, Franklin Delano Roosevelt, was struck down by what at the time was thought to be polio. While historians now believe he may have suffered from the Gullain-Barré virus—his much older age and bilateral paralysis are unusual for polio—the impact on him and the lasting damage were not. Despite efforts to find a cure by soaking in the healing waters of Warm Springs, Roosevelt was never able to walk without the aid of braces and strong arms to lean on again.

Roosevelt's background, wealth, and connections allowed him to focus efforts on research and education, hoping to understand the mystery that was polio. Forming a group to raise money to support those efforts, Roosevelt persuaded an attorney friend, Basil O'Connor, to take over the reins of The National Foundation for Infantile Paralysis once his condition stabilized and he was able to return to pursuing his earlier political ambitions. The Foundation's mission was not only to provide funding for prevention of and finding a cure for polio, but also to provide financial support to care for those affected by the disease.

Initially holding an annual Birthday Ball in honor of Roosevelt's birthday and raising much-needed funds, O'Connor quickly realized he needed to broaden the donor base if the work of the foundation was to continue. Rather than relying on a limited group of wealthy socialites, he came up with the idea of raising small sums of money from huge numbers of people, something that had never been tried before.

Vaudeville star Eddie Cantor, playing on the well-known March of Time newsreels theme, suggested creating thirty-second radio appeals and coined the phrase 'March of Dimes.' Public announcements were soon heard everywhere, increasing donations beyond O'Connor's wildest dreams.

"A dime; anyone can contribute a single dime. Everyone has a dime to spare."

Encouraging children to donate a dime became the rallying cry of the organization, and the results of their efforts were noted as enormous bags of the tiny coins began inundating local post offices. Dimes gathered in classrooms and on street corners, anywhere people might pass by and donate, poured into the White House. The name, March of Dimes, while synonymous with the organization in people's minds, did not become the foundation's official moniker until 1976.

The March of Dimes covered all the costs of my illness. I cannot imagine what would have happened had they not been there for my family. Struggling simply to make ends meet, my parents could never have afforded my three-year hospitalization, in addition to doctors' fees, therapies, numerous surgeries, and other expenses that lasted far beyond my time at Pittsburgh Children's. Most families, like mine, had limited resources; health insurance was still a fairly new concept and not widely available, especially for the self-employed. The donations made across the country, one dime at a time, spared thousands from bankruptcy, or worse: being denied care.

With a cure for polio appearing unrealistic, efforts to control the disease focused on prevention. In 1935, following a successful experiment with monkeys, immunizations were given to a group of children, which proved to be a disaster when several of them died and many were left paralyzed. This tempered enthusiasm for further trials and led to some of the major debates between those favoring a vaccine using a dead virus versus one containing an attenuated, or live, but weakened one.

Hilary Koprowksi, a researcher at Wistar Institute, developed the first oral polio vaccine using the attenuated virus in 1948. Easier to administer than injections, and believing an oral vaccine was more effective — targeting the intestinal tract directly where the virus multiplied and entered the bloodstream — he tested it on himself and twenty residents of Letchworth Village, a home for mentally disabled children in New York. Seventeen of the twenty developed immunities to the virus, and the other three were believed to already have had a natural immunity. Koprowski's attenuated virus was used as the basis for the later Sabin oral vaccine.

Epidemics in the US were occurring with greater frequency. In 1949, 2,720 people died and another 42,173 were affected. The epidemic of 1952, the worst in American history, killed 3,145 of the 57,628 cases reported, and left 21,269 with mild to severe paralysis. The urgency to find a vaccine intensified, as did the arguments over using the inactive or active virus, with most researchers favoring the attenuated version. Fierce competition raged as well between the leading proponents of each approach, Jonas Salk and Albert Sabin.

Salk, an advocate for the inactive form, was the first to bring a mass producible vaccine to the public. Unbeknownst to anyone or allowing for any oversight, he tested it on himself, his own family, and nearby institutions, the DT Watson Home for Crippled Children and the Polk State School. In 1953, he published a paper with his results, unleashing a furious debate over the safety of the vaccine and the ethics of his methodology.

His greatest defender appeared in the person of Basil O'Connor, the head of the March of Dimes. O'Connor's adult daughter, a mother of five, had contracted the disease. Fearing another widespread epidemic, he directed the foundation to fund a trial, this time a legitimate scientific study.

Commencing in the spring of 1954, over 1.8 million children participated in the program. A full blind study, no one knew whether the vaccine they received was real or a placebo. Some of the children, found later to have received a faulty batch that contained traces of the live virus powerful enough to cause polio, contracted the disease. Following the trial, general immunization programs were instituted, and the overall rate of new infections plummeted over 80 percent in two short years, a smashing victory in the war to eradicate the killer.

Meanwhile, efforts to produce a safe, effective vaccine using the live virus continued. While the inactive form prevented the spread of the disease, it did not provide lifelong immunity, and flare ups continued to occur. Albert Sabin, Salk's primary detractor, worked around the clock perfecting his vaccine using the live virus, which he knew was the only way to create the lasting effects that could potentially lead to the ultimate eradication of polio.

In 1959, finally ready to test his results on children, he travelled to Russia, a country that had been experiencing continual outbreaks and had yet to have a widespread vaccination program. Over 10 million children received the oral vaccine, and its success was irrefutable. In addition, the Sabin vaccine was found to cause an active infection of the bowel, which, when excreted, could help protect those who had not been otherwise immunized.

National Immunization Days were soon common throughout the country. School children were marched into the cafeterias or gymnasiums, and waited in long lines, their parents eager for them to finally have a weapon in the fight to combat the dread disease.

The Salk injected vaccine, administered through mass inoculation programs beginning in 1957, and the Sabin oral vaccine, administered by placing drops on a cube of sugar to mask its bitter taste beginning in 1962, dramatically curtailed the spread of the disease. By 1961, the number of reported domestic cases had dropped to only 161, and the last recorded cases of endemic polio in the US occurred in 1979 in small Amish communities in several Midwestern states. The battle to eradicate polio in America had finally been won.

Unfortunately, it came too late for me.

1948-1949

Doctors Thomas Weller, John Enders, and Frederick Robbins
successfully grow poliovirus in live tissue culture,
paving the way for the creation of the polio vaccine.
Six years later they receive the Nobel Prize for their work.

CHAPTER 3

My eyes, riveted on the doorway, kept watching for my parents to walk through any moment. I'd barely slept the night before, waking at the slightest noise, wondering if morning had come. My nurse teased me playfully as she gathered my few belongings into the tiny duffle bag that now sat on the chair next to me in the hospital waiting room. "You won't miss us a bit, Bobby; you'll forget us in no time, you'll be so happy at home.

"They'll be here any minute. Sit up straight and stop wiggling. You want them to see how well behaved you are, now don't you?" the nurse continued.

When my parents were finally allowed to visit me, I was almost eighteen-months-old and no longer remembered them. The trauma of separation had been hard on them, depending solely on letters from the nurses and occasional phone calls from the doctors to keep them updated regarding my progress. They sold their home in Texas and returned to Bloomsburg to be closer to family — and to me — once they were allowed to visit. Hiding their anxiety from everyone, they kept busy with work and caring for my sister, and although they lived over 200-miles away, once the visits were permitted they made the round trip to see me monthly without fail. Slowly, over the next two years, I reconnected with them, a buried part of me reawakening as I remembered the sound of my mother's voice or the feeling of my father's arms as he lifted me up to say hello. Their visits ended far too soon, and the days between them felt like an eternity. Each time they left I sobbed, begging them to take me with them.

During their visits, my mother sat on my bed and told me stories about my sister Ginnie and my grandparents who lived nearby. My father brought a small metal chair in from the hallway, squeezing it into a tiny space next to us in the crowded ward where he could listen to the two of us talking. Occasionally he chimed in with a story about a piano he was working on or a fishing trip he and my grandfather had just taken. Sometimes my mother simply read a book, her voice falling gently over me as I imagined the stories coming to life, particularly the ones where boys could run and play with abandon.

This time, when my parents came I wasn't going to hear the words, "We'll be back as soon as we can, Bobby." This time, I was going to go with them, walking out the doors by myself, one step at a time just like I'd been practicing with the therapists for many months.

Trying to contain my excitement, I kept looking at the door. I heard their footsteps first, my mother's high heels so different from the nurses' soft rubber soles. I put my crutches under each arm and pulled myself up. I wanted to be standing when they walked in.

Finally, they came around the corner. My mother spoke first.

"Hi, Bobby, are you ready to go home?" She reached out to greet me, and I froze. She was somehow different from the woman who visited and read to me; something was wrong.

"What's going on, Bobby?" the nurse asked as I hid behind her. "You're going home with them today; it's a great day for you!"

"I'm scared," I whispered in her ear. "She's scary." Peeking

28

around, I looked at my mother, transfixed. I had never seen her face uncovered. I had never even seen my own face in a mirror.

Fearful of contagion, everyone in the hospital, including visitors, was required to wear masks and gloves. Other than Robert, the kindly chocolate-skinned gardener who lived in the outside world filled with fresh air and sunshine, I had not seen anyone's full face unmasked, and his was only from a distance. He'd wave at us through the glass windows as he passed by, maintaining the grounds near our ward.

"It's okay, Bobby, it's still your mom!" the nurse encouraged me, nudging me gently toward the woman who stood stoically, waiting for me to move toward her. Torn between my desire to hide and my longing to go home, I swallowed hard to conquer my fear and took a tentative step toward her waiting arms.

"Bye, bye!" I cried, turning to give my nurse one last wave.

"We're so happy for you. You'll love being home!" she waved.

Leaving behind all that I had known, I slowly walked out the door, taking my first steps outside as I headed to a place I had only heard about in stories.

"How do I get in?" I asked my dad. "Where do I sit?" I'd never ridden in a car before.

"Come here by me," my mom directed, patting the back seat next to her. "Let Pop help you," she said as he took the crutches from under my arms and lifted me up. Placing my bottom on the seat, he unlocked the rigid brace at the knee, allowing it to bend. I could turn myself, fitting easily in the giant space. But the window was too high. I couldn't see anything except the seat in front of me.

"I wanna see!" I cried. My hospital memories were limited to white: nurses and doctors in their crisp uniforms, bleached bed sheets and blankets, and plain drab walls. Eager to take in all the new sights, I begged my mom for help to reach the window.

"Let's see what we can do, Bobby. We might have something in the trunk that will help you." My dad went to the back of the car. I could hear the opening of the trunk and the rustle of things moving. A few moments later I felt the car shudder as he slammed it shut.

"Here you go, son," he said, reaching through the door with a pillow in his hand. "Lean over and I'll push it under you and lift you up. That should help you see better." The pillow elevated me just high enough that I could peer out the side.

"Make sure your hands are out of the way," he instructed before closing the door securely and climbing into the front. Starting the engine, he put it into gear. I was going home.

"What's that over there, Mommy? What's all that noise? Why is everybody outside? What are those kids doing?" My brain on overload, I peppered my mother with my incessant questions and running commentary. Picture books couldn't capture the intensity of the colors, sounds, and aromas I was suddenly experiencing as we drove west to Bloomsburg. Car engines roared and horns blared as we drove through traffic, and the smell of newly mowed grass permeated the air. I kept staring at the texture of the different trees as they blew gently in the breeze. Kids played in parks, laughing while they chased each other. Dogs barked, running after balls tossed by their owners. There was something to see no matter where I looked, and I wanted to take it all in.

"Wake up, Bobby, we're here." My mother's gentle voice broke through the fog of sleep. I had dozed off somewhere along the highway, overwhelmed and exhausted.

So this is home, I thought, noticing the house with a young girl standing on the front porch. "Is that Ginnie?" I recognized her from the small picture my mother often pulled out to show me. I had no memory of her, and she had never been allowed to visit me in the hospital. I hadn't seen her in over three years, and while my mother always told me how much she missed me, in reality, we were complete strangers.

My father helped me out of the car and stood me on the ground. Bending down, he secured the brace at the knee. I adjusted my crutches under my arms, and began slowly walking up the front steps where my mother had gone to wait for me. All the while Ginnie kept staring at my legs.

"He walks funny," she whispered to my mother. "Will he get hurt?"

"No, Ginnie, he will need some help at first but he will be just fine. You can show him around the house if you'd like. He needs to know where his bedroom is. Can you take him there now?"

I look back sometimes and wonder what life had been like for her. In her seven short years our parents had divorced and remarried and a sister died from crib death. Her baby brother got sick and was sent away. She was uprooted and moved from Texas to Bloomsburg, and now her brother, no longer the baby she remembered, was coming home. Through it all, our parents, typical of their generation, were silent, offering only the simplest explanations along with clear expectations to probe no deeper.

It took some time for us all to adjust to my being home. It was quite a change from the hospital, where nurses took care of all my needs, though I was often left on my own when they tended to other patients. My parents, particularly my mother, had to learn what I was capable of and what help I needed. I had to learn what was expected from me and what I was allowed to do on my own. Ginnie had to figure out where she fit into this new family picture.

Some things settled easily into routines. Waking up in the

morning, it was obvious I was helpless to do anything for myself and had to wait for my mother's arrival to get out of bed.

"Okay, Bobby, time to get up and dressed!"

"I can sit up myself!" I protested as she cheerfully came over to put her arm behind my back and lift me forward. "I'm not a baby!" Stopping, she watched as I pushed myself up with my arms. "See, I can do it!" I crowed, as I leaned back against the wall, my stomach muscles too weak to hold my body upright without support.

"Yes, you sure did. You ARE a big boy! Now, arms up!" Pulling my pajama top over my head, she slipped on my shirt for the day. Next came the bottoms. "Use your arms to lift up so I can tug these off. That's right." Wishing I could do it on my own, I watched as she rolled up my pants and pushed my shriveled foot into the opening before repeating the same movement for my slightly more cooperative right leg. Other than retaining the ability to feel sensations such as hot or cold, my left leg was completely useless.

"Now use your arms to scoot back against the wall again while I get your braces ready." The heavy metal contraptions required first strapping a wide leather corset across my waist. Buckling it tightly gave my torso the support it needed to hold me upright.

"Let's do your left leg first." Waiting for me to recognize right from left, my mother used every opportunity to teach me. She expected me to learn quickly and retain the knowledge, quizzing me throughout the day on colors, numbers, and spelling.

Reaching down and lifting my twisted, skinny, and visibly shorter leg, she placed the steel metal brace on either side and slid my foot into the boot attached at the bottom. She tied the laces and cinched the straps all the way to my hip, securing it in place.

"Now the right leg." Fitting the boot onto my foot, she

tightened the partial brace around my calf. Without the support, my foot flopped down and dragged on the ground. Keeping it rigid gave me one usable leg.

"Meet you in the kitchen for breakfast!" My mother smiled, then turned and went down the hall. I reached for my crutches, slid to the side of the bed, and stood up. Taking a moment to balance, I placed a crutch under each arm and began the slow walk through the house, my hunger propelling me forward.

Ginnie watched, fascinated, as I put the crutches in front of me, and using my hip for momentum, swung my left leg forward. The brace, locked securely, provided enough stability for standing while I propelled my right leg forward. I walked exactly as the therapists at the hospital had showed me.

My first few weeks at home were exhausting. I was more physically active than before. In the hospital most of the time was spent sitting in a chair reading, doing physical therapy exercises, or in bed. Unaccustomed to the sudden lack of restrictions, I wanted to do everything, but my physical stamina couldn't keep up with my mental curiosity.

"Come sit down and look at these books, Bobby. I know you want to play, but you have to give yourself time to get better. Leaving the hospital doesn't mean you are completely well yet, only that you are ready to finish getting better here at home with us."

Like any other youngster, I wanted to explore and move. I loved being outdoors and went roaming any chance I could. My mom's insistence that I take frequent rest breaks was irritating, but she was right. I rarely napped, but I did get tired easily.

"Mom, come help me." In the hospital the nurses insisted we wait for them before we did anything, fearing we might be injured if we weren't careful. Typical of a four-year-old, I wanted to do a lot of things by myself, but I had also learned to be overly dependent on others. When I first got home, I frequently asked for help with things a child my age could easily do alone.

"No, Bobby, you can do this yourself," was often my parents' reply.

"No, I can't!" I whined back as they ignored me. My parents were determined to treat me as normally as possible, forcing me to struggle until they were certain I actually needed assistance before stepping in, wanting me to figure things out. Frustrated at first, I grew increasingly determined to do things alone and soon refused most offers of aid, as much from stubbornness as self-sufficiency. I especially hated it when it was Ginnie trying to help. Four years older, she often acted like a second mother to me.

"Come here, Bobby, I hafta help you. You're just a baby.

"No Bobby, you hafta do it my way.

"Bobby, I'm gonna read to you, you have to let me. I'm bigger than you."

"Let me alone, I can do it myself!" Ginnie was treating me like a child, and I resented it. I was a big boy, not one of her dolls. At the same time, she was also my first playmate, and I wanted her company.

"Hey, wait for me! You're a meanie going so fast!

"I wanna go pet the horses next door; I don't wanna play dolls!"

Before long we were fighting like normal siblings when she came to realize I wasn't fragile and wouldn't break. No longer an only child, Ginnie complained about all the attention I required. I, on the other hand, decided no part of the house was off limits, including anything that belonged to her. Following my sister everywhere, I loved bugging her as much as I loved having her companionship.

"Tell Bobby to leave my toys alone!" echoed constantly throughout the house.

My confidence grew along with my strength. My desire to have someone to play with pushed me harder to keep up with Ginnie.

"Look at me, Mommy!" I yelled from the front yard. "I can go fast now! Come watch me!" She came out on the front porch and watched me race back and forth across the grass, demonstrating my latest discovery. Frustrated trying to run with Ginnie, the method I'd been taught at the hospital for walking was far too slow for an active boy. Instead of taking one step at a time I swung both legs together. "See, I'm running!"

"Why yes, you are!" My mother's smile was encouraging. "Just be careful you don't wear yourself out now," she continued, turning back toward the house. "You still have to do your chores."

"Wait, Ginnie, I fell. Wait!" Once more an unexpected tree root tripped me. Flying face first onto the ground, I spit out a mouthful of dirt before looking around for the nearest boulder I might use to help me stand up. I crawled over, dragging the rigid brace, pushing as best as I could with my right leg and tossing my crutches ahead of me. I grabbed the rock with both hands and pulled myself up until I could get my crutches back beneath me. Catching my breath, I took off after her again.

Observing our play from the kitchen window, my mother had seen enough. *There must be an easier way for Bobby to get back up. This is ridiculous.*

The next day, borrowing crutches from a friend, I watched as she took a few steps, fell carefully to the floor, and sat on the ground thinking.

"Well, Bobby, what if I put the crutches under my arms first, then pulled myself up?" she said, more to herself than me. She immediately ascertained that the leverage she needed to get up wasn't there. "No, that won't work. What else can I try?"

She experimented for quite some time, until stumbling upon a solution. "Here you go. Put both crutches together on your right side, like this," she demonstrated as she described what she was doing. "Now, push up on them at the same time you use your left leg for balance and your right leg to help you stand."

I sat on the floor, mimicking her actions. It took several attempts before I was able to master the technique.

"Now then, Bobby, you should be able to get up anywhere all by yourself," she announced, very pleased with the knowledge that she had given me one more step toward independence. Each milestone meant I was getting better.

"Mommy, I hate this thing. I don't wanna to wear it; it hurts," I tugged at the leather belt around my stomach. Unfortunately I still needed the corset, but listening to my complaints prompted my mother to improvise ways to strengthen my body.

"Sit in the swing and use your tummy to hold you up," she guided me. "Hold on tightly with your hands to keep you from falling." Pushing one hand gently against my back while pressing her other one against my stomach, I could feel what she wanted me to do. For hours, I swayed gently in the yard under the shade tree and practiced as hard as I could.

Adding sit-ups to our routine was another attempt to strengthen my body. My mother sat on the floor with me and held my feet while I strained to pull myself up. "One," she counted as I fell back, exhausted. "Tomorrow we'll do two." Each day she added another until I was easily able to do twenty without complaint.

"Bobby, it's time to see if you can walk all by yourself without the corset," my mother announced as she came in to help me dress. "We're going to leave it off today." Finishing our normal morning routine, I stood up, grabbed my crutches, and took a few tentative steps toward the kitchen.

"Look, Mommy! I can do it!" Clapping happily at my success, she followed me down the hall. I never wore the dreaded corset again.

Polio is an extremely painful disease. Often distracted by day while I was busy playing, my body tormented me when I went to sleep. I woke up most nights in tears, crying for my mother. "Everything hurts. My arms are all achy inside. Make it stop!" Every inch of my body burned, almost as if I had a blinding migraine in each of my limbs.

"I know, Bobby, I know it hurts, honey." Unable to ease my pain, my mother sat by my bedside for hours, brushing away my tears. "Let me read to you. That will help you think about something else besides your pain. Would you like to hear one of the stories from my newest comic book?"

Never wanting her to go away, I always said yes. Her favorite, the comic horror book series *Tales from the Crypt*, filled my head with terrifying images that came back to haunt me in my sleep.

Awaking with a fright, I looked frantically over the edge of my bed, hoping my screams had scared the skeleton that was hiding there. I was certain he lived under my bed, waiting only for me to nod off before reaching up with his long, bony fingers to drag me to my death. Still too young to tell the difference between fact and fiction, I believed that if it was on paper, it must be real. In my nightmares, my mother's stories came vividly to life. My parents, asleep in their room, hadn't heard my desperation. Alone against evil, I put my head back down on the pillow, clutching one of my stuffed animals tightly to my chest, my eyes canvassing the room until sleep once again overtook me.

Other nights were no better. When neighbors came over to play canasta, my mother's instructions were clear: don't bother us with anything other than a true emergency. "You and Ginnie can watch TV as a special treat in the next room. I expect you to behave and not cause any problems."

Ginnie, four years my senior, controlled the channels, and she liked horror movies.

"I don't like this," I implored. The shows terrified me. I wanted her to change the channel to something I preferred, but she saw this as an opportunity to lord her age over me.

"I'll tell everyone you're just a scaredy cat." Challenged, I was compelled to watch with her just to prove I wasn't a sissy.

Predictably, canasta evenings were followed by sleepless nights filled with horrid dreams. My mother never figured out why I insisted on sleeping in the middle of my bed with the covers pulled securely around my neck until I left home at nineteen. My fear of things lurking in the dark lingered far longer.

~

"When do I get to go to school like Ginnie?" In the kitchen one morning, I kept begging my mother to let me go. Even though it was summer, I watched Ginnie getting her supplies ready, putting pencils in the small zippered pouch and filling her notebook with lined paper. I wanted my own book bag. I wanted to go off with the big kids. Since I'd come home she'd been teaching me reading, writing, and arithmetic, and I was a quick study. "I can read already; I want to go!"

"Well, you're five now, and it's time for you to start kindergarten. You'll be going along with the others when classes resume in the fall." I was going to be going to the same school as Ginnie! I felt very grown up.

"Listen to the teachers, and be quiet in class." My mother issued her final instructions as I got out of the car. "Sit in the circle with the others, keep your hands to yourself, and play nicely. I want you to walk with Ginnie and she'll take you to your class." She waved goodbye and watched me enter through the front doors.

Barely outside for my first recess, I was tackling the ladder for a third time when the playground monitor started yelling at me. "No young man, you can't go up there! Come down right away!" she scolded. "You must sit over here by me where you won't be hurt."

Why would I sit during recess when the other children were playing? Of course I didn't listen. Turning back to the task at hand, I pulled myself up another rung before she came over and grabbed me. "I'm taking you to the principal right now!" She jerked me down, and holding my collar, marched me into the office, ordering me to sit on the hard wooden chair while she reported my crime and the principal called my mother. Still not understanding why I was in trouble, I could only wait until she showed up to set things right.

"I don't understand. Mom. Why won't they let me play with the other kids?" I cried when I saw her. "I didn't do anything wrong. I was just going on the slide with everyone else in my class." My sister and I played outside constantly at home, climbing, running, and fighting. My body was the only body I had ever known and in my memory I always had polio. I never felt limited in what I could do physically, only challenged to figure out a way to make it work for me. Suddenly I was being treated differently than the other children. My parents didn't limit me; who were these strangers telling me I couldn't do something I felt perfectly capable of doing?

"Mrs. Mutchler, please come into my office. Bobby, you can come in as well," the principal instructed. Following him through the open door, we sat in chairs across from his desk.

"What exactly is the problem?" my mother inquired. Like me, she wasn't sure why I was being singled out. "Has Bobby injured someone? Did he get hurt?"

"He has disobeyed our teachers. He was told to stay off the slide and refused to listen. We cannot guarantee his safety around the other children, and I believe he will be better served by homeschooling," the principal announced as if his decision were perfectly obvious. "We just can't have that here. He makes the other kids uncomfortable and they are afraid they may hurt him. We will send out a teacher to work with him tomorrow."

"This isn't about his safety," my mother retorted. "It's about your discomfort with his physical appearance. He plays on everything at home; we've always treated him as an able-bodied child." My crutches and braces were a reminder for many of what damage polio wrought, and fear was still widespread. Claiming a concern for my safety was an easy excuse. There were no laws in place to protect my placement in class. Knowing she had no other options, my mother grabbed her purse, stood up, and looked the principal directly in the eye.

"Fine, we'll expect him in the morning." My mother's clipped voice barely contained her anger. "Bobby, let's go home." We walked out the door without a backward glance. My kindergarten days were over.

The homeschool teacher was pleasant enough, but when my mother saw that his idea of an education was playing tic-tac-toe, she sent him away and resumed my lessons herself. I spent hours lost in stories of far away places, immersing myself in adventures I could only dream about. Reading anything I could get my hands on, I devoured every childhood tale before moving on to the adult classics. With no other distractions, I progressed at my own pace in all subjects. I had an excellent memory and could easily recite facts and figures, doing math equations in my head. Never required to show my work, I quickly learned that knowledge, not busywork, mattered.

What I missed was playing with other children. My only friend was Ginnie, and I never learned the intricacies of social interaction. My relationship with my sister was based primarily on learning how to bug her just enough to get satisfaction, though not so much as to have her stop letting me tag along. For the first time I experienced being singled out because of my polio, and I felt a seed of anger taking hold inside of me.

Pop and me—only 3 days old—on his Harley (1947)

Mom on her Harley in Texas (1947)

Ginnie and me in Bloomsburg (circa 1951)

1952

The worst U.S. epidemic of polio on record: 57,628 cases reported.

1953-1954

The inactivated, injectable, polio vaccine, developed by American
medical researcher Dr. Jonas Salk, is tested on over 1,830,000
children between the ages of six and nine. Albert Sabin begins
official testing of 'live,' or attenuated, oral polio vaccine
in Chillicothe, Ohio.

1955

Salk's vaccine is declared safe, potent, and effective. Immunizations
commence, and within two years cases of polio in the U.S.
decrease by over 85 percent.

CHAPTER 4

My grandfather, Harold Parker Mutchler, otherwise known as HP, was a local bootlegger, hunter, fisherman, and expert poker player. He was also one of the most successful businessmen in the small town of Bloomsburg, Pennsylvania. Welcomed into the highest social circles despite being 'simply' a piano tuner, he raised ten children. My father, Bob, was the eldest of the eight born to his first wife, my grandmother, who died long before I was born. When World War II broke out my father enlisted in the Merchant Marines and served as a warrant officer until his discharge. Coming back home he followed HP's career path and set up business as a piano tuner.

Returning to Bloomsburg following my polio diagnosis, my father branched out into the freight business, buying three long haul trucks and hiring drivers to cover the routes he was establishing. Finding success in this new endeavor and sensing a bright future, my parents bought a small home and two cars, matching Nash Ramblers. The business continued to flourish, and I spent the first two years post hospital reacquainting myself with my family.

"Bob, can I borrow the truck this weekend for a side job?" A good friend of my father's was at the door. "I'll get it back early Monday, clean and ready in plenty of time for your driver to load it for his route." Always one to help someone in need, my father readily agreed. The friend, and the truck, never returned.

The loss of the not yet paid for truck and the income it produced devastated my parents' finances, leaving them with few options. In bed in my room I overheard their conversations late at night when I couldn't sleep. Although I didn't understand everything they were saying, I understood the tension in their voices.

"I refuse to declare bankruptcy; I'd rather die first. I will figure out a way to pay these debts, and clear my name and reputation. No one will ever believe in me otherwise. Dammit, we have no choice!" I could hear the anger rising in my father's voice, followed by the crash of something breaking against a wall. I'd seen him hit my mother before and I was afraid he was so angry this time he might again. Another time I witnessed him grab her while they were arguing in the kitchen. I watched, terrified, as she jerked her arm and he let go. She turned and walked away without saying a word. While his violence was infrequent, it was unpredictable and his sudden outbursts and loud voice were frightening. He rarely struck my sister or me, but once I came home I learned to stay out of his way when he started yelling, because when he did hit it hurt. His temper petrified me.

My mother, attempting to calm the situation, offered solutions.

"Throwing things won't fix anything, Bob. We need to come up with a plan. We can sell our house and live in a trailer; I don't care. We'll do whatever we have to do.

"We can get rid of a car.

"We can move in with your parents.

"We'll go wherever the money is for as long as it takes. What's important is we work together to figure this out."

I kept quiet, afraid to let on I'd heard their argument. In front of Ginnie and me they acted like nothing was wrong, but a few days later my father came home with a tiny, beat-up Cozy travel trailer and announced we were going on a trip.

"Pop wants to try his hand at different jobs, and we're going to go with him," my mother announced with an artificial cheerfulness. Typical of my parents, this was all the explanation we were given.

"Can I take my cars?" "What about my dolls?" Ginnie and I pestered our parents, hoping to bring as much as we could into the cramped caravan.

"You can each take two toys. Pick them out and put them in the trailer. The rest will be at Grandfather and Grandmother's when we come back," my mother's voice was clipped. "Here's a box to pack them in." Allowed to take only the barest necessities, I said goodbye to the rest of my things as I shut the lid, shoving the small brown package toward my mother.

In the backseat with Ginnie, I pressed my nose to the window and took a last look at our little house. My grandparents waved goodbye from the front porch as my grandmother discreetly dabbed her eyes. My father put the car in gear and pulled away from the curb, not knowing when, or if, we'd return.

~

For the next two years my father changed professions often, moving us to a new location if he heard of something more promising. Selling life insurance, driving a combine during harvest season, repairing and tuning pianos, dynamiting things as a demolition expert; no job was beneath him. Often working three shifts a day, we sometimes went weeks without seeing him. My mother contributed, too, selling cookware, bibles—any other item she could. They sent every extra dollar home to repay their debts.

Too young to understand the hardship my parents were experiencing, my sister and I saw this time as a grand adventure. My only awareness that money was tight was the food we ate. Picking raw fruit off the ground in soon-to-be harvested orchards, I grew to hate the taste of oranges and grapefruit. My mother, expertly stretching a dollar, created a million and one uses for hamburger, and oatmeal mush was a morning staple. My stomach still recoils at the thought of putting either one in my mouth ever again.

Our living situations changed with every move. For the first several months we stayed in our trailer, finding camping accommodations near whichever town offered work. It wasn't long, however, before the Cozy was being packed up and my parents had a new plan.

"We're selling the trailer and moving into a tent," my father announced one evening after dinner. "I'm going to build a small cargo frame to put our things in to tow behind the car. Ginnie, you and Bobby will sleep in the car while Mom and I share the tent."

With no further explanation, we moved our belongings into our new home. Our 1940s era Dodge had plenty of room for me in the front seat and my sister in the back. Taking the few cooking utensils that fit in the small spaces remaining, my mother simplified her menus to what could be prepared over the small wood fires in the campgrounds we found near wherever my father had work.

For a brief while we lived in a rented cottage on the beach in Daytona, Florida. Ginnie and I spent hours every day playing along the shore.

"Wait for me!" Yelling at Ginnie to slow down, my crutches kept sinking into the soft sand. Frustrated and angry, I stopped, looking for anything I could grab to throw at her. Her delight at my predicament was even more infuriating.

"Hahaha! Can't catch me!" she taunted, running just out of reach. "Why don't you come in the water with me?" she shrieked, peals of laughter carrying across the expanse of beach. Diving into the warm ocean, she surfaced only long enough to continue her tormenting. "Come on in, Bobby; it's so nice in here!"

"I hate you!" I muttered under my breath, stopping when I finally neared the water's edge. Easier to navigate, my crutches found more resistance in the wet sand, but fearful of actually getting in the water, and knowing the weight of my braces would cause me to sink, I watched, helpless to ever catch up to my sister when she wanted to keep away. Turning my back on her, pretending she didn't exist, I plopped down just out of reach of the lapping waves.

I scooped the damp sand and began sculpting a castle. The beach, full of small shells, inspired my design. Soon lost in a fantasy world of knights and dragons I didn't hear Ginnie approach.

"Can I help?" Fascinated, she resisted her normal temptation to stomp it into oblivion. "I can add a tower for the princess over here." Hours passed, arguments and teasing forgotten as our miniature world absorbed our attention.

Like many of our homes, the beach cottage, too, was temporary. We soon moved on when my father found work in Mobile, Alabama, and where my parents apparently found religion.

"Amen! Hallelujah! Praise the Lord!" I watched the people around me raise their hands, speak a garbled language foreign to my young ears, and fall to the ground, overcome by emotion. My mother soon joined in. *What was going on?* Confused by the sudden change in my normally staid parents, I was both appalled and fascinated by the behavior of the adults around me.

"Stop staring!" Ginnie slapped my arm. "It's rude!"

"What are they doing?" I whispered. "Why are they talking so funny?" In my seven years I had never seen the inside of a church, and the fervor of the Pentecostals was starting to scare me. Never noticeably religious before this, my parents were now constantly dragging us to Sunday worship services and Wednesday prayer meetings. I had my doubts. "This is goofy, Ginnie. I don't get it."

I attended various churches throughout my childhood, but never did understand the comfort my parents found in religion.

Moving yet again, we were back once more in our tent, staying briefly in a campground in rural Oklahoma. Ginnie and I played outside by day and climbed into our beds in the Dodge at night.

"Wake up, kids! We have to get out of here right this minute!" The urgency in my father's voice woke me from a deep sleep. I could hear the winds shaking the trees in the dark. "Scoot over NOW!"

"What's going on? What's happening?" Ginnie sat up and rubbed her eyes as my mother ripped open the door. Shoving my sister across the bench seat, she jumped into the car and slammed the door.

"A tornado's coming. We have to get away. We have to get out of here RIGHT NOW!" Pop's voice yelled over the increasing noise of the wind. Gunning the engine, he pealed out of the campground, driving as fast as I'd ever seen him go. "It's coming from the west so we're heading south. No real place to hide; we have to hope to escape its path."

I'd read about tornados in one of the books my mother had given me, and I knew Oklahoma was one of the states where they occurred. I felt a mixture of fear and excitement as we barreled down the two-lane road. Not fully comprehending the damage they caused, I wanted to see one close up. But my parents' anxiety was contagious, and I was always afraid of my father's temper. I kept my mouth shut, silently watching the sky outside my window.

After what seemed like hours, my father pulled off the road. "It must be gone by now," he said, turning his head to talk to my mother sitting behind him. "Let's go back and see what's happened to our camp." In our haste to escape, they'd left the tent with all our gear inside.

With the sun coming up, the trees cast shadows throughout the small park we had been calling home the past few weeks. Branches were scattered across the open grassy areas, and I spied an upended picnic table against the swing set I had been playing on only the day before. As we neared our site, I noticed something hanging from the tree Ginnie liked to climb. It was our tent, shredded beyond repair. Our small cargo trailer, dumped on its side, was halfway across the street, clothes scattered along the ground.

"Now what?" my mother sighed. "What else can happen?" Her voice cracked. It was one of the first times I heard her come close to crying. Usually brisk and uncomplaining, she stood, surveying the damage.

My father, uncharacteristically, put his arm around her waist. "We'll figure it out," he reassured her. "We'll figure it out."

Righting the trailer, my parents pushed it back across the road to our campsite while Ginnie and I gathered the belongings we could reach, stacking them in a pile to be sorted later.

"I think there's enough canvas left I can fashion a tent to cover the trailer. We can sleep there and the kids can still stay in the car." Ever resourceful, my father went to work creating our new home. Not long after, we moved on to another town, another state, and another job.

"Now this will be perfect," my father proudly announced, showing off our latest acquisition, an old converted school bus

51

he'd found in a junkyard. "Almost like our old trailer." No matter what we lived in, they made it feel like home, and I developed the ability to sleep anywhere.

~

Walking through the men's locker room with my father, I proudly carried the small bag filled with swim trunks and a towel. The pool was housed inside the Omaha, Nebraska YMCA. Sitting on the steps in the warm water, I loved splashing with my hands and putting my face forward until it sank below the surface. I blew bubbles and held my breath as long as I could before popping back up, sucking in the moist air of the indoor pool.

"I can get myself in the pool, Pop," I insisted. "I don't need you to help me. Watch." Sitting on the hard wooden bench, I unlocked the knee of my left brace, allowing my leg to bend before reaching down to untie my boot. I undid each buckle and let the metal lean against the bench as I lifted my leg and let it drop down before tackling my right boot. Slipping out of the short brace, I pulled off my pants and tugged my swimsuit up until I was ready.

I grabbed a crutch under each arm and stood, balancing cautiously on the wet cement. Swinging my legs together, I made my way slowly to the edge of the pool where I sat carefully on the slightly raised lip. I placed my crutches where I knew I could easily reach them when I was ready, then scooted off the side to the top step.

"See? I told you I could do it." My father's pride was evident as he helped me slip my arms into the life jacket my mother insisted I wear and tightened the belt around my waist.

The warm water was soothing against my bare skin. My father watched as I slowly inched down to the second step, lowering myself just far enough until my legs began to float. Content that the vest would keep me above water, he took off and began his methodical exercise. Taking a break every now and then to check on me, he was soon lost in his own world, secure with the knowledge the lifeguards would save me if I ran into a serious problem.

Wanting to imitate the other swimmers and no longer satisfied merely dipping my face in the water, I decided I was ready to go completely under. The vest was an impediment, keeping me from sinking, and it had to go. I checked to see that my father wasn't looking, then undid the two straps that held me in. Setting it on the side of the pool, I wiggled back down the steps until my whole body was immersed, only my head above water. I held my breath, pushed myself off the last step, and sank to the bottom. I was underwater!

When I couldn't hold my breath a second longer, I shoved up with my arms, bursting through the surface and scrambling to find the step. Gasping for air, I made sure my father was still oblivious to what I was up to. My breathing back to normal, I sucked in a bunch of air and plunged in again. Over and over I sank to the floor of the pool, pushing up again at the last second.

"Why is your vest on the side of the pool?" my father's booming voice caught me by surprise. "What the hell do you think you're doing?"

The first day had ended successfully as I'd been able to strap the life jacket back on before my father noticed. Now I was caught red-handed.

"I've been teaching myself to swim." Looking him directly in the eye, I knew lying would get me into far more trouble than telling the truth. "While you've been doing your laps, I've been practicing holding my breath." I kept talking, hoping to convince him not to yell at me.

"After I learned how to go underwater, I started swimming like the fishes do. I don't need my legs to make me move, I can use my arms. Here, let me show you." I pushed off the step before he could stop me. Just as I had described, I began wiggling my whole body, pushing my arms out in front of me and pulling them down to my side. Underwater, I moved freely, only popping my head up when I needed air. "See, Pop, I can swim. I don't need the vest anymore," I announced proudly, my demonstration complete.

He stared at me. As he contemplated how to respond, I watched him closely, his unpredictability often confusing. He was at times attentive and taught me things, taking the time to show me the correct way to bait a hook when we were fishing or wanting my help to set up camp. At other times he was stern and demanding, expecting instant obedience. I was never sure when his temper would flare and I would become the object of his anger, yet he exhibited pride in my accomplishments and wanted me to be treated as a whole person, not a cripple.

"Don't you dare tell your mom," he demanded. I breathed a sigh of relief. Thankfully, this time pride won out over anger or his promise to my mother. My worst fear was that although she never came to the gym, she would somehow discover our little secret and force me back into the life jacket, her anxiety of me drowning inhibiting my brief moments of freedom.

Teaching myself to swim, I was finally free of all constraints, no one telling me I couldn't do something. My father watched from across the pool, his silence tacit approval of this step toward independence. I savored every minute, knowing all too soon I would be back on dry land, dependent once again on cumbersome braces and crutches.

~

In the early 1950s, the US was comprised of 48 states, and we visited all of them before I turned nine. We camped for weeks in some of the most beautiful state and national parks long before they were overrun with tourists. I caught my first fish, a trout, in a lake north of Boise, Idaho, an event made even more memorable because everyone else came up empty-handed. Cooking it over the fire that night, in true fisherman's form, I told the story of the catch over and over, embellishing all the small details.

Ginnie and I played endlessly after school and during her breaks. The parks we stayed in offered adventure wherever we turned, and the outdoors were our playground. Our parents shooed us out of the campsites in the mornings with a snack to carry for lunch, and didn't expect to see us again until dinnertime.

Our latest game, throwing stinging twigs at each other to see who could inflict the largest welt, was both torturous and hilarious. As long as I had a moment to plant myself, I could use one of my crutches to deflect her attacks. She was defenseless; in her haste to escape often flung her hand out only to be hit by the flying branch.

Crossing the stream, I misjudged the stability of a rock I chose for my next step. Usually it was my crutches sinking in the soft mud that caused me to stumble. "I swear when I catch you I'm going to whip you!"

"Sure, I'll wait for you," she taunted. "And while I'm waiting, let me smack you one with this!" she laughed, gleefully whipping me with the biting leaves.

My sister and I occasionally met other children in similar circumstances, and we roamed the forests, inventing games and exploring nature. Even if the parents were uncomfortable with my body, when Ginnie was around, their kids had no choice but to include me.

"Did you ever see what the inside of a slug looks like?" the boy from the neighboring campsite inquired. "Let's cut one open and see!" Gathering around, we watched, fascinated, as he pulled out his pocketknife and began slicing the slimy green creature.

"Booooring," was our consensus. "It looks the same inside as out." Other science experiments, made up depending upon what we found in our surroundings, were often more interesting. Guessing the animal from skeletal remains, following unknown tracks, or pouring salt on unsuspecting slugs and watching them writhe and wiggle provided daily entertainment.

~

"Bobby, what in the world do you think you are doing? Get down this instant!" My mother came up behind me unexpectedly and startled me.

Losing my grasp on the rope, I slid to the ground, scraping all the skin off both my hands and injuring my foot.

"I bet you won't dare do that again," she said as she poured the antiseptic over my wounds. "That should teach you."

I held my tears, never complaining while she scrubbed the dirt away, biting my tongue rather than admit she might have been right. Of course, as soon as my injuries healed, I headed straight back to the rope, determined to make it to the top.

"Don't go to the drugstore by yourself. No playing pinball on the machines," was an invitation to do the exact opposite. As soon as my mother turned her back, I'd return to whatever I was doing. Hearing 'you can't' was a challenge to prove 'yes I can, just watch me.' I was becoming increasingly rebellious, kept in check only by a fear of being caught and punished by my father. Aware of his temper, my mother often kept my misdeeds from him.

~

My parents were always searching for medical procedures that might help me regain some functionality in my body. It wasn't uncommon to hear different ideas from different doctors. I hated the appointments, having strangers poking and prodding me. They spoke to my mother as if I weren't even in the room or as if it weren't my body they were discussing cutting into.

"We think transplanting a bit of muscle from a part of his body that is still working into the damaged leg will restore some movement."

"We need to take some bone out of his knee to help it bend better."

Sometimes their ideas resulted in surgery, other times my parents ignored their advice. I had no say in the matter, merely informed on the mornings I was taken in for procedures and expected to be happy they were trying something to make me better.

"Mrs. Mutchler, after examining Bobby, I think it would be best if I amputated his left leg. It's not serving any purpose and he'd be better off without it. My opinion is based on the latest ideas for treating the aftereffects from polio." My mother had brought me into the local doctor hoping to get some advice for my continued physical therapy while we were on the road. "I have an opening for surgery next week. We can take care of this right away."

"Mom, no!" I cried, tears welling up in my eyes. "Don't let him touch me!" As useless as my leg might seem to him, it was a part of me, and my brace gave me the ability to move. What would happen if it were gone? "Take me home; please, Mom, please!" I begged.

"It's okay, Bobby. Thank you, Doctor, but we're not interested in amputation. I don't believe that is the answer I was looking for." Gathering her purse and nodding to me to stand up, we started to leave. "Shake the doctor's hand, Bobby." Stunned that my mother had listened to me, I eagerly complied.

My legs were not the only parts of my body affected by polio; they were only the most visible. I struggled with breathing, the disease having damaged my diaphragm. The therapists at Pittsburgh Children's Hospital taught me to use my stomach muscles to help me breathe, but when I got excited, or my attention wandered, suddenly I'd be winded, as if I had just finished a race. I had to force myself to consciously slow down, relax, and take several long, deep inhalations before I could get going again.

~

At first, as we moved from town to town, my parents enrolled me in the local schools. I was put in a Special Education class during a short stay in Savannah, Georgia, the principal somehow confusing my weakened legs with a lack of intelligence. A teacher in Kansas City, Missouri, spent weeks on the intricacies of long division, something I had mastered by the time I was seven. I thought the teacher's demand to show my work was ridiculous. I refused to do my homework and argued when confronted with my 'laziness.' I wasn't lazy; I was unchallenged and bored. Having read every book in the school library I thought writing a book report was a waste of time. At first I wasn't disruptive, I just made the others uncomfortable, but over time I stopped caring about trying to fit in or please the teachers.

While my sister attended the local school and my parents worked, I spent most days by myself. My mother and father no longer had the time or energy to engage small town principals in a battle to have me enrolled in their schools only to have me kicked out on some silly pretense within days. While I occasionally attended classes, it was often easier to leave me at home with books to read or arithmetic problems to solve, written out for me on small scraps of paper. The campgrounds we stayed in were often home to other families in similar circumstances and there were usually adults around in an emergency.

I missed playing with Ginnie when she left for the day. Pretending not to mind, I waved goodbye to my family as they left each morning, but the anger that had started in kindergarten kept simmering with each incident where I was made to feel different. Though my family treated me as an equal, the rest of the world didn't. I was still a reminder of the ravages of polio, which made people uncomfortable when they saw me.

Despite my anger at being left out, I was used to being alone. I taught myself to figure out problems in my head and loved tricking my mother. When she started scolding me for not finishing the math problems she'd left me that morning — sure I had been goofing off—I blurted out the correct answers. The stories I read fueled my imagination. In my pretend world, I could run through open meadows, soar with the eagles, and dive to the bottom of the ocean, freed from the chains that were my braces, my body strong and whole. In my fantasies, I had friends and was invited to be on the best teams, admired for my strength and coordination. In my imagination, polio didn't exist.

1957

Sabin's oral vaccine is tested on children
in Czechoslovakia and the Soviet Union.

CHAPTER 5

It took two years for my father to pay off his debts. During that time we made our way west, reaching California in time to celebrate my eighth birthday. We purchased a small caravan in a local trailer park near Sacramento and settled in, where my parents were befriended by a local family, the DeLoziers. When they offered us a place to park our tiny home on their property, my father accepted. Adding a second equally well-worn trailer, we now had space for Ginnie and me in one, and my parents in the other. Pastor De Lozier, a minister of a small congregation in town, let us stay for nearly a year, during which time my father bought a small music store and Auburn became our permanent home.

My father's business acumen and his decision to hire Henry Vande Graaf, a local musician, helped the store become a huge success. Henry could play any instrument set before him, and my father could repair any instrument that required servicing. Word swiftly spread. Feeling financially stable again, we moved from the tiny trailers to a real house. The music store also introduced me to my first, best, and lifelong friend, Jerry Allaway. His mother was a frequent customer and eventually became my mother's close friend. The two of them, along with another local musician, formed an all-women's country western trio and played gigs around town.

~

"Bobby, I have a surprise for your birthday. We're going to Los Angeles. You, Mom, and Ginnie will spend the day at Disneyland while I attend my meetings." My father was on the board of the National Music Merchants Association, and he had various committee meetings in Los Angeles every month. This was the first time he was including us in his plans.

"What's 'Disneyland'?" I inquired. While much of America had watched the opening of the park just weeks before on television, Ginnie and I were rarely allowed into our parents' bedroom where they kept their tiny black and white set. We had missed following the stars into the different 'lands,' each with its own rides, stores, and adventures.

"It's a giant amusement park," my father explained. "You'll see. They have rides on stagecoaches, miniature cars, a rocket ship to the moon, and a voyage beneath the sea. I'll drop you all off and come back when my meetings are over. We'll leave Friday after I close the store."

Los Angeles was almost five hundred miles away. A trip of at least ten hours by car, we drove past cotton fields, over the mountain pass between Bakersfield and the San Fernando Valley, through small towns and into Anaheim. Ginnie and I slept most of the way, waking just in time to see a bright yellow billboard, complete with a cartoon mouse driving a smiling train alongside one of the seven dwarves with "Disneyland, 3 miles ahead' in giant letters.

We pulled into a huge parking lot surrounded by orange trees. Across the lot I saw a line of families waiting to purchase tickets. A giant mouse face, formed only from flowers, greeted us. Just above him was a railroad station, and I could hear the whistle of the approaching train. From the outside, it looked a lot like many of the county fairs we'd visited in our travels across the country.

"Here are your entrance tickets. Kids, listen to your mother. I'll come find you later," he instructed, handing my mother money for rides and lunch. He turned to leave.

"Have fun and be good!" he yelled over his shoulder, waving as he walked back to the car.

My mother gave Ginnie and me each a dollar. "You'll need to buy tickets for the rides, which cost between ten and twenty cents each. There's no more money when this is gone, so you'd better think carefully how you want to spend it. Let's go inside and decide where to start."

Through the Magic Tunnel, we walked onto Main Street, entering a turn-of-the-century town complete with horse-drawn carriages and organ grinders with their dancing monkeys. I'd never seen a fair quite like it. At the end of Main Street I spied a castle. The scene was busy with people and shops. I stopped in the middle of the street, taking it all in.

"Bobby!" My mother's sharp warning brought me back to the sound of a clanging bell. Turning, I had just enough time to scoot out of the way of an approaching cable car. "Bobby, you need to watch where you are going!"

"I want to go to Fantasyland." Ginnie's decisiveness carried the moment. "I want to go on the rides there. The map says it's straight ahead, through Sleeping Beauty's Castle. I want to ride on the Carousel." We headed up the street, this time on the sidewalk, peering into the shops filled with candies, clothing, and various other sundries. Perhaps we'd look inside later, but like Ginnie, I wanted to try the rides.

We crossed the moat and walked under the walls of the castle, arriving at another world. To my right was the Peter Pan Flight.

People sat in miniature pirate ships waiting to enter the opening to a medieval-looking building just ahead.

"Mom, I want to go on the Peter Pan ride." I was hoping I'd get to meet Peter, having read the stories of his escapades in my books.

"That's fine. Go get your tickets, and we'll get in the line." Ginnie was just as eager, and we soon found ourselves flying through Wendy's nursery, over downtown London, and on to Neverland. We saw moving figures of Captain Hook, Princess Tiger Lily, and others, but no Peter. My mother explained we were supposed to be viewing the scene as if we were Peter himself, flying over the countryside. I was enthralled by the entire experience, the magic of the characters, and found myself totally immersed in the adventure. In that moment I fell completely in love with Disneyland.

~

"I need to go to Los Angeles every month for these meetings. Would you and Ginnie like to go with me and spend the day at Disneyland while I take care of business?"

I looked at my father to see if he was joking. Did he really think we'd say no? "Yes, Pop, yes!" I squealed. "Of course I want to go!" Ginnie was equally enthusiastic in her response.

Once a month we packed into the car on Friday night, falling asleep shortly after leaving only to awaken as the sun came up and we were pulling into the parking lot. I never grew bored with the Magic Kingdom. For me, it truly was magical. Believing the park was probably one of the safest places in the world, my mother began accompanying my father to his meetings, dropping Ginnie and me at the front gate. Left on our own, we split up, exploring every square inch of the park. Our parents usually found me on

Tom Sawyer's Island. We spent Saturday nights at the Sands Motel across the street, endlessly debating which rides and which 'land' was the best, then awakening early Sunday for the return trip to Auburn, the excitement of the day before often lulling me to sleep most of the way home.

~

"Bobby, it's time for you to go to regular school. I know you may be ahead of the other students academically, but you need to learn to get along with other kids, and how to behave in class." After we settled in Auburn, my mother had continued to homeschool me, but I was getting older, and my parents decided things needed to change. They knew I struggled with fitting in, and wanted me to have a chance to finally make friends.

The first day of class proved to be just as disastrous as all my previous experiences.

"Time for recess, children. Everyone line up at the door and I'll take you outside. Johnny and Danny get the playground balls, and Sally, grab the jump ropes. Susie, you bring the beanbags. Remember you are also responsible to bring them back when the bell rings." As instructed, I lined up with the other students to go out to play.

"Oh no, Bobby, you need to remain inside for recess and physical education. It's not safe for you with all the kids running around, and you can't do the activities anyway. You just stay in here and read. It will be much better for you." The teacher's condescending voice boomed above the scraping of chairs and the shuffling of feet.

I felt my face turning red, anger and humiliation rising up in my throat. The other kids began to snicker, whispering to each other behind their hands. I stared at the teacher. Did she really mean it?

She nodded her head emphatically. "Sit, Bobby. I will expect to see you in your seat when we come back in."

I turned and went back to my desk. Grabbing my book, I buried my face in the pages, pretending not to notice as they filed out of the classroom. But once I knew they were safely outside, I grabbed my crutches, hobbled over to the window, and watched them playing kickball, tetherball, flag football, and tag. I could hear the silly chants of the girls as they took turns hopping in and out of the line jumping rope. Others tossed their beanbag markers on the hopscotch outline, holding their place as they clicked their heels jumping from square to square. I longed to join them, yet hated them for their cruelty. With tears starting to well up, I turned my back to the playground, sat down at my desk, and opened my book. Already far ahead of the class academically, I was now expected to spend even more time studying. Every day as they left the room I pretended not to care.

Increasingly frustrated and bored, I began snooping around the classroom. I opened the tote bag of one of the other students, reached inside, and felt what seemed to be a metal object. I pulled out a miniature car, painted red and black with wheels that moved when I rolled my fingers across the tires. As I slipped it into my pocket I experienced a slight thrill and before the class returned I was back in my seat, deeply absorbed in my novel.

The next day, once the class was safely out of the room, I waited a few minutes before taking a chance and rifling through a second bag, justifying my actions as a reasonable response to them excluding me. This time, I found a small piece of candy, tightly wrapped in foil. Shoving it into my pocket, I returned to my desk and my book. If they were going to make me stay in during playtime, then I was going to at least find a way to have some fun on my own. Toys and candy weren't allowed in school, and while it was apparent the kids knew something was going on, they were too afraid to tattle, fearing getting into trouble themselves. I didn't care if they suspected me since they didn't include me in anything anyway. I began to view stealing as both a challenge and as payback for the way I was treated.

~

"When are you going to learn to listen?" My mother's exasperation was evident in her voice. Apparently there had been another conference with the principal. "If your father got these calls your backside would black and blue. I can't understand why you just can't do what the teacher wants you to do."

"The teacher wants me to show how I solved the math problems and I did them in my head. She wants me to write a book report on a stupid book I read two years ago. She isn't interested in what I know, only in how I fill out the worksheets." Why couldn't my parents understand how frustrating it was to sit in a classroom where everything went so slowly all I wanted to do was scream just to ease my boredom?

"Well, I'm not homeschooling you anymore; you need to be around other children and learn how to get along. Your father and I discussed it. You're going to private school, no arguments. Maybe they can beat some sense into you." She stood up and walked out of the room.

Without consulting me, they had apparently already made the arrangements to enroll me at Pine Hills Junior Academy, a Seventh Day Adventist institution. When summer ended that fall I found myself walking into a new school for the start of seventh grade.

Students were a little bit friendlier and my first few days were positive. Although I still wasn't invited into most games during recess, I was allowed to go outside with the class. I spent most of my time wandering around the playground by myself, ignored by the others, which was at least preferable to being teased. I was still

67

far ahead academically, and the school didn't have a way to differentiate the subjects to sufficiently challenge me. Still, I tried my best to fit in and behave.

Kids brought their own lunches, and my mother often packed eggs for me from the local geese, chickens, and ducks. One morning before leaving home, particularly frustrated with my teacher for making me complete a ridiculously easy assignment the day before and forcing me to show my work when it was obvious I had the correct answers, I grabbed a raw goose egg. I tucked it into my jacket pocket and waited for the perfect opportunity for retaliation.

The ringing bell signaled the end of lunch and the beginning of recess, and as the line of students spilled out onto the playground, I veered off toward the restroom. Reaching the door to the boy's room, I checked to make sure no one was watching before sneaking around the corner of the building. I knew our teacher stayed in the classroom for most of the break until heading into the main building to pick up mimeographed worksheets; her predictability would be her downfall.

The roof along one side of the building was just within my grasp. While my legs were weak, my upper body was very well developed, and I knew I had the strength to pull myself onto the school roof using only my arms. Hiding my crutches behind a trash container, I reached up and took hold of the eaves. *Here goes nothing.* I gripped my hands on the lip and pulled myself up, listening to the shouts and laughter of the students on the playground. *Good, I still have time,* I thought, using both arms to pull myself over the eaves and onto the flat surface. Lying for a moment to catch my breath, I knew I had to hurry. I crept to the edge of the building, took the egg out of my pocket, and peeled the paper off I'd placed around it to keep it from breaking. I peered over, waiting patiently. A moment later I heard the door opening. Yes, it was the teacher! I let the egg fall from my hand, timing it perfectly to hit her on the head. I hastily pulled myself back from view, and listened for her reaction.

"Oh my goodness, what was that? A bird must have hit me! Oh, dear, what a mess!" she cried. "I need to get this cleaned up right away before it stains." I heard her footsteps as she hustled off to the office, laughing silently until tears filled my eyes. I took a few moments to celebrate my cleverness before scooting back to the other side of the roof. Sliding back down carefully, I hung on until my feet touched the ground. Then I let go, landing with a thud, the stiff brace on my leg keeping me upright. I bent over to pick up my crutches from their hiding place, slid them under each arm and turned, rejoining my classmates on the playground before they noticed I had been gone. Success! I hadn't been caught.

Back in class, I sat quietly in my seat, trying my best to focus on my studies. I was startled when the teacher singled me out. A student helper from the office was standing next to her, and I could see a crumpled note in her hand.

"Bobby, come up here right now!" Her stern voice conveyed her disapproval of me.

Uh oh, does she know something? What's in that note? I smiled meekly in my attempt to maintain an innocent expression.

"Young man, come with me. We're going to Mr. Funkhauser's office. I believe you have something to answer for," she continued, grabbing me by the collar and steering me through the door. "Don't even think you are going to get away with this."

Standing in front of the principal I tried my best to convince him he had the wrong boy. "Mr. Funkhauser, I didn't do anything. I was on the playground with the other kids. I don't know what you are talking about," I pleaded.

"Oh, were you now?" His tight, thin smile indicated he knew I was lying. "Too bad your friend Johnny saw you on the roof and let me know what you were up to," his smooth voice turning brittle. "Come with me; we need to have a little chat."

I quietly followed behind him as he pushed his wheelchair down the walkway to a small storage room. A former professional baseball player who had been in a terrible car accident years before, I knew I wasn't going to arouse his sympathy. He opened the door and invited me to enter. Pulling the 'Board of Education' paddle from its special holder on the wall, he placed it on his lap and looked at me.

"You may believe you are a clever young man, but God sees all. It is our duty to help you understand the sinfulness of your actions. Drop your trousers and bend over." Wheeling his chair to my side, he picked up the paddle and began his methodical spanking. "One. Dear Lord, please help Bobby see the error of his ways." Swat. "Two. Help him become a good Christian boy." Swat. My backside stung with each stroke as the paddling continued. I held my breath and bit the inside of my lip, determined not to give him the satisfaction of seeing me cry. "Thirty. Thank you, Lord, for guiding me in saving Bobby's soul."

The spanking finally over, I pulled up my pants carefully, wincing as the cloth scraped my burning skin. He returned the paddle to its holder. "Bobby, we want you to be successful here. I hope this little episode won't be repeated.

"Now come with me; we need to call your father." I dreaded my father's wrath more than any paddling. Standing by the office door, I watched Mr. Funkhauser pick up the phone and dial. "Perhaps your father will want to discipline you further when he gets home."

"Mr. Mutchler, I need to inform you of Bobby's misdeeds." The principal's tone was as serious as his facial expression. "As you know, our punishments include paddling. I gave him thirty whacks with the wooden board. With each stroke, I prayed for his soul, that he might see the light and abandon his sinful ways. It's possible the blisters left behind may be a reminder to him to seek good."

I watched as the conversation concluded, wondering what lay in store when I saw my father later that evening. I was terrified I might have gone too far this time. I went home and spent the rest of the afternoon sitting on my bed, dreading his impending arrival.

My father and I were never really close; we did many things together and had happy times, but he was most often a strict taskmaster. Occasionally, he erupted in physical violence toward my mother, my sister, and me. Despite my overall lack of respect for authority, I was intimidated by him, and never argued with him until I was an adult.

While hating his anger, I also respected his drive to clear his name and to take responsibility for his debts, and I absorbed his lessons. As a teenager, I didn't appreciate that he was probably tougher on me because he wanted me to be a survivor, like him. My mother tended to be more protective, often colluding with me by not telling my father some of my worst misdeeds, and standing up for me when his anger was out of control. I appreciated her support, but I also learned to manipulate her good nature whenever I had the chance. With my father, there was no getting around him once he decided I was in the wrong. On more than one occasion he told me to do something, and I failed to do it to his satisfaction. Coming into my room in the middle of the night, he'd wake me up, drag me out of bed, and sit, watching, until I finished the task to his standards. My mind drifted to an earlier incident when I had disappointed him.

"Bobby, I want you to change the tires on the trailer. We're going to the other side of the mountains on Saturday and we'll be pulling it behind us."

71

A typical ten-year-old, a bit lazy and careless, I did a poor job of securing the bolts. Driving over Donner Summit in California in the middle of winter, our car began lurching side to side.

"What the hell was that?" my father yelled. I jerked my head around just in time to see one of the tires from the trailer bounce off the curb and sail over the edge of the cliff. Still swearing, he steered the car off the road, put it in park, and turned off the ignition. Everyone sat still, not knowing what was coming next. My father took a few deep breaths, shook his head, and turned to me.

"Bobby, let's get out of the car and have a little chat." Now eerily quiet, my father waited while I grabbed my crutches and my jacket and climbed out of the warmth of the back seat. I had no idea what he'd do next.

"Have a seat here, son. I don't want anyone to take it," he commanded, pointing to a spot on the trailer away from the road. "Don't you dare move, and don't you dare talk to anyone." He got back in the car and drove off, taking my mother and sister home, leaving me to sit on the side of the road shivering in the cold. Returning an hour later with a new tire, he made me put it on while he watched. I was no 'poor Bobby' in his eyes.

The slam of the car door brought me back to the present. My father was home and I had to face him. As much as I wanted to, I couldn't hide in my room forever.

Bobby! Get out here!" The knot in my stomach tightened. "NOW!"

"Let me see the damage," he demanded. I dropped my pants and waited. He stared for a few moments before speaking. I waited, afraid to say a word, afraid to give him any more reason to be angry with me.

"Impressive!" I could hear the admiration in his voice for the thorough job. "I don't believe I need to do any more. I think the pain you feel sitting for the next few days will teach you a lesson," he concluded.

I couldn't believe my good fortune; I wasn't going to be yelled at or spanked. "I promise I'll be better. I promise I won't make the principal mad again." My words were heartfelt and sincere. I meant to be good, but of course, I wasn't always able to match my intentions with my actions.

My blisters healed and the bruises faded, but my anger at my punishment festered. I wanted to get even but fear of what my father would do if I got caught again kept me in check. Biding my time, I waited for an opportunity.

Months passed. Finally another boy was caught misbehaving, briefly overshadowing my misdeeds. Lying low, I tried my hardest to listen to the teacher, although I still thought she was making me do stupid work. Now that the attention was off of me, I decided the day had come for revenge.

Making sure Ginnie wasn't watching, I went into my room and closed the door. I pulled a ratty cardboard box out of the back of my closet, sat on the floor, and peeked inside. *There're still here, good.* I picked up the tiny dynamiting caps that I found when my father was still working in demolition, knowing someday I might find a use for them. I wasn't sure how he had used them, but he had mentioned once that they produced 'a small, contained explosion.'

I hid them inside my jacket, returned the box to its hiding place, and opened my door just far enough to make sure no one was watching. The path was clear. I walked quietly to the back door and slipped outside. My mom would assume I was playing with friends so I had time to take action.

The school was only a few blocks from the house. Teachers left shortly after classes ended, and I knew the janitors finished their work an hour or so later. Trying to look nonchalant, I first walked around the entire block, glancing sideways to confirm the school grounds were deserted. Then I moved briskly across the parking lot and slid between two of the yellow buses parked in a neat row. It took only a minute to decide the best placement. Just at the front edge of the back tires, I concluded. They blended in with the ground; no one would notice them there. Moving from bus to bus, I stuck a cap snugly against each tire, close enough to be hidden with just a bit of space to prevent setting one off if I pushed it too far. When I finished, I took a second to admire my handiwork before heading back home in time for dinner.

"I need to get to school early tomorrow, Mom. I have to meet a friend to finish a question on my homework," I lied. I wanted to be there in time to observe the results firsthand. The hedge across the street from the parking lot was the perfect hiding spot. Knowing the caps would detonate on impact, I had only to wait a few minutes before the bus drivers came out to start their routes.

"Kaboom! Bam!" The explosions even louder than I had imagined, I put my hand over my mouth to stifle my triumphant shrieks of laughter from bursting forth. *"Boom!"* *"Blam!"* I had carefully chosen the buses I knew would move first, and as I watched, the tires exploded in rapid succession just as I had hoped. Lurching to a stop, the bus doors flew open and drivers jumped out, running around trying to figure out what had caused so many tires to fail at once. Luckily, all the evidence was destroyed along with the tires or my father probably would have figured out I was the culprit. I finished out the remainder of the school year satisfied I had been able to exact my revenge.

~

"Ginnie, let's go for a ride." I invited her to join me on the horses our neighbor allowed us to use on occasion, taking them in easy circles around his enclosed yard. The back section, covered in thick Manzanita bushes, didn't have a fence, but the horses never wandered to that portion of the yard.

"Hey, look; there's a break in the bushes. I wonder if we can fit through." Ever curious, I wanted to see where it might lead.

Later, through the back door, I overheard the clipped tones of my mother's voice. "I see. Yes, we'll talk with them," and the click as she hung up the phone. "Children, come in here this minute!

"That was the neighbor. He just got home after wandering all over looking for his horses. Did you realize you were teaching them to escape? Weren't you told explicitly to stay in his yard?" Her voice rose in anger. My father came into the room to see what was causing the commotion. It was unusual for her to be the one demanding punishment.

"Bobby, you go with your father. Ginnie, you come with me. You're both getting a spanking." Reluctantly, I led the way to my room, my father behind me, slowly unbuckling his belt. I knew what was coming, and knew it was pointless to argue.

Closing the door, my father sat down on my bed. "Listen, son. I'm just not in the mood for spanking tonight, but your mother needs to believe you've been punished. You scream loud enough and she'll be happy I whipped you hard."

I stared at him. Was he serious? I couldn't believe what I was hearing. I was happy to comply, and soon my father was snapping his belt loudly against the mattress while I yelled at the top of my lungs. I loved sharing the secret with my father, knowing the occasions he took my side were rare.

1958-59

Sabin's vaccine is field tested,
proving the live, attenuated vaccine is effective and safe.

CHAPTER 6

"This has shown promise. I think his theory makes sense." I could hear the hope in my mother's voice as she presented the doctor's most recent recommendation to my father. "I think it's worth a try. At least he's not suggesting we cut off his entire leg like that last guy!"

I didn't want any more surgeries, but no one was asking for my opinion. Whatever procedure they chose I had to endure.

As the day for the operation approached, I felt a familiar dread mixed with a slight optimism; perhaps this really would be the miracle that would let me walk better. Finally I was wheeled into the operating room and a mask was placed over my face. For a brief second I smelled the ether as the nurse encouraged me to breathe comfortably, and then the world went dark.

"I can't move! I'm trapped!" As the anesthesia wore off, I tried to turn in the bed, but couldn't. "The polio's back! I can't breathe!" I kept screaming, frantically waving my arms as I tried repeatedly to sit up.

"I'm here, Bobby," my mother's voice was reassuring. I hadn't seen her in the room. She walked over and put her hand on my arm, pushing it back down on the bed. "Your arms are free but you're in a body cast to keep everything in place while you recover."

"Why didn't you tell me? Why do I have to do this?" I whined. It was typical of my parents not to say anything to us, but it would have been nice to be warned. "How long will I have to be in this?"

"We didn't want to scare you. You'll be able to move just fine when it comes off in a few months." While pleasant, her voice indicated the questioning was over. I knew when not to argue.

"It hurts. It itches!" I wanted to rip off my skin, but I had no way to get to it. Pain was a constant companion. "Can't they do something to make it better?" My mother simply sighed. There wasn't anything 'they' could do. I was stuck in bed, immobilized. At least I was at home.

"I went to the library today and picked up more books for you in addition to the ones your teacher is requiring you to finish. If you keep reading at the rate you're going you'll be through the entire *World Book Encyclopedia* before you get out of that cast." She piled the latest stories on my bedside table. "I'm off to work. Ginnie will be home at three. If you need anything, you can call but don't use the phone unless it's really an emergency," she instructed. "Your teacher also left you several pages of arithmetic problems. I'll check your answers after dinner." Smiling, she waved goodbye. I listened as the front door closed. I was alone, left to my own devices for the next several hours.

Picking up a book, I was soon lost in another world. When my arms tired of holding the heavy novel, I put it on the bed beside me and picked up one of the assigned math sheets. I swiftly dispatched with the easy homework, then challenged myself to solve far more complex problems in my head using an imaginary chalkboard. Though my teachers seemed to find it so annoying, this was the way I always liked doing math.

Tired of equations, and determined to avoid the required reading as long as I could, I closed my eyes. Songs began playing in my mind, their notes dancing before me. My family was often singing and the sounds of my mother's guitar were a constant wherever we lived. It was fun to try and write my own songs, composing simple melodies at first. Over time, they became more complex.

"I'm home!" Ginnie's voice burst through my consciousness. Another day had passed, and I had filled it with an amazing amount of activity, all while flat in bed. What initially felt like an eternity flew by and soon it was time to return to the doctor, remove the cast, and see if anything had changed.

I was hopeful while we waited for the doctor to saw off the plaster. "You won't be able to do much at first. You've been still for so long that it will take time to get things moving again. We won't know for a few weeks." I looked down at my legs, fresh from their imprisonment. They were even scrawnier than before, my skin flaky and scaly. It didn't inspire much optimism.

As with all the other procedures, it was soon clear nothing was different except I now had new scars to add to the many others. I was tired of being poked and prodded, and told my parents I didn't want any more surgeries. Thankfully, this time they agreed. In the meantime, I had missed enough school that between this lengthy absence and my general unwillingness to turn in assignments, the school decided to hold me back a year, forcing me to repeat seventh grade. The Adventists, to their credit, never gave up on me, and while never fully conforming, I did complete a sufficient amount of work to finally graduate eighth grade.

~

"Please let me go to Placer High. I want to go to public

79

school." I'd been begging my parents for the past year to free me from the confines of a religious environment, and I could sense I was starting to wear them down. "It's cheaper and they have a good music program." They finally agreed.

I wanted a fresh start, to have new friends and not be identified as slow, lazy, or a troublemaker. I wanted to fit in, to understand how to talk to girls, to sit together and maybe sneak a kiss on the cheek. I wanted to be challenged academically. I had great hopes for Placer High, but instead, I was once again excluded from many activities, made to do homework I felt was beneath me, and set apart from my peers.

I took on the role of the class clown, talking loudly, making jokes at the teacher's expense, and garnering notice from the others, but never genuine acceptance. I presented a tough guy 'I can handle anything' exterior to the world. In many ways I really didn't care about others, having only felt pity and ridicule from them, never empathy. I was on the outside looking in, though occasionally someone chiseled through that toughness, exposing a deep hurt even I didn't know was there. Most often I responded with anger, my hair trigger an attempt to keep me from shedding unexpected tears. On the rare occasions when they did break through, it angered me even more. It was much easier to act out than to try to fit in. When I couldn't find a logical outlet for my anger, my sister was a convenient, and frequent, target.

"Hey, Ginnie, I've got your favorite record. I'm going to play it and you can't stop me!" I teased. She hated when I touched her things. I'd had another lousy day at school and she was the perfect distraction.

"I'm going to kill you if you do!" she screamed, running down the hall from her room. "I swear I'll make you pay!" Grabbing a knife from the kitchen drawer, she came into the living room where I was sitting on the floor holding her precious 45.

"Go ahead and try," I dared her.

She let it fly. I had no time to move, only time to watch as it sailed across the room and landed smack between my legs barely half an inch from my crotch. It stuck in the wooden floor, wobbling a bit before coming to a stop. I waited a full minute before reaching over and pulling it out, studying the sharp blade.

I looked up and smiled sweetly at her. "Oh dear, you missed. Better luck next time." Infuriated, she stormed out of the room, slamming the door.

No innocent bystander herself, she was always looking for ways to get me into trouble, usually doing something devious and blaming it on me.

"Bobby, why did you leave this mess in here? I told you to clean up when you were finished! Get in here right now and pick it up. No arguing, NOW!" I didn't dare disagree with my father when he went on a rampage. Just out of his line of sight, Ginnie stood grinning slyly from the corner of the kitchen. We both knew she had made the mess. She had gotten her payback.

~

I made a few friends at Placer, and in my music classes I was at least respected for my abilities. As always, I was restricted from physical education classes, and spent the hour in study hall reading on average a book a day. My best friend, Jerry, and I were finally in the same school now that I had transferred, and although we rarely had classes together we hung out in the afternoons and on weekends. One day, I urgently needed to use a toilet.

"Hey, Jerry, let's use the one in the school. I don't think I can wait until we get home."

"Bob, it's Saturday, the school is closed. Everything's locked."

"When has that stopped me? Come on, it'll be fine." We walked around the empty building, juggling door handles to see if one had accidentally been left open, and came to a small service door with a simple lock. "I can pick this," I stated with confidence. "This kind is easy."

Jerry kept watch as I pulled a penknife from my pocket and inserted it into the lock on the door. It was as simple to open as I had predicted. Quietly pushing it open, I entered the building. "Come on, Jerry. Wait in here so no one sees us. I'll be right back."

The door led to staff offices. No public restrooms in this part of the school, but I'd been to the principal's office enough to know he had a private bathroom and kept the key to it in his top desk drawer. I walked over and opened it, searching until I found the key with the tag 'bathroom' attached.

"Bingo! Got it!" I whispered loudly to Jerry, still standing guard in the hallway. I unlocked the small door in the corner that opened to a private bathroom, and went inside. After, I returned the key to the desk drawer, and, closing it tightly, re-joined Jerry, making sure the office door shut securely.

"Let's get out of here," Jerry insisted, anxious to leave. Peeking through the windows at the end of the hallway to make sure we were still alone, we crept back outside.

We started toward home breathing a sigh of relief. I was leading the way and didn't notice Jerry was no longer following. I turned around to see empty space behind me. He must have gone home. His house was before mine, so I assumed he had turned off when we neared his street and I hadn't heard him say goodbye.

Thirty years later, Jerry confessed. "Remember that day we broke into the school? I was behind you and stopped to tie my shoe, and you just kept going. You always thought I went home right away. Well, I didn't. One of the teachers saw me leaving the building and grabbed me. He asked if I was alone or if someone was helping me. I never let on you were there. Boy, did I get it when I got home!"

A loyal friend, he never snitched and he never told me, knowing I'd be forced to confess, unwilling to let him take the punishment alone.

1962

Sabin's vaccine rapidly becomes the vaccine of choice for most of the world, proving to be not only easier to administer but providing longer-lasting immunity.

CHAPTER 7

My grandfather dumped the parts onto the garage floor. "If you can put this together, you can ride it." He looked down at his ten-year-old son, curious to see if he'd accept the challenge.

"I can do this," the young boy responded. "Just watch me."

Within weeks, the reconstructed motorcycle finished, my father was riding everywhere. Demonstrating his gift for all things mechanical, he kept the bike in excellent repair. As a teenager, his passion for riding only intensified. Imagining a life of adventure, he left home at fifteen and joined a circus, spending a summer displaying his talents alongside clowns, acrobats, and animal trainers. He thrilled audiences in the aerodrome as they watched him drive his Harley Davidson up a flight of stairs, flip it around on the small landing, pop a wheelie and fly back down. But as exciting as it was, he soon tired of the road and returned home to learn the family trade, piano tuning.

But he never lost his love of motorcycles. After settling in Auburn and watching the music store become a success, he expanded and opened a Honda dealership, which was ranked the number one motorcycle dealership in the Western United States three years in a row, proving his business acumen wasn't a fluke. Clearly, I had my father's aptitude for mechanics, as I spent much time in the shop, and easily learned how to build and repair bikes.

I'd ridden on the back around town with my father, but by the time I was thirteen, I wanted desperately to take a bike out alone. I envied the teenagers who came in to try them out, the ease with which they could swing their legs over the seat, and, riding off, shift with their left foot while using their left hand for the clutch. Most importantly, their legs provided the balance needed to keep the bike upright when it came to a stop.

"Pop, is there any way I can ride by myself?" I asked repeatedly.

His answer was always the same. "I'm sorry, Bob, this is one place your legs may always hold you back. I could figure something for shifting, but I can't do anything for the balance. You have to be able to hold the bike up. Maybe someday something will help, but I'm not aware of anything yet. At least when you're sixteen I can teach you to drive a car."

The local sales manager for American Honda, Derrick Lee, called my father one day and asked if he'd be willing to evaluate a prototype they were working on. I wasn't in the shop, but he told me about it.

"It's an interesting contraption. Honda wants to see if it will sell. I know a guy is thinking about buying it, so we'll get his feedback."

After tipping over on only his second ride, the man returned the next morning, demanding a refund. There were dents and scratches on the side where it fell, and my father knew it'd be hard to re-sell used. I still hadn't seen it so had no opinions; I was barely even listening to him while he pondered how best to make use of it.

My attention had been focused on Christmas, which was rapidly approaching. I loved the holidays, seeing all the lights and decorations, and I eagerly anticipated the excitement of discovering what goodies might be awaiting me in the morning. Always awakening well before our parents, my sister and I raced into the living room to see what was under the tree.

But this year something was different. Rummaging through the boxes, I couldn't find any with my name on them. While never expecting many gifts, it was clear there weren't any for me. Never greedy for toys, I was still surprised. *That's odd. Why didn't I get anything?* I couldn't understand why I'd been forgotten, but I knew better than to say anything. Instead, I sat quietly, watching my sister and parents open present after present until none were left.

Trying to hide my disappointment, I pretended to be interested in Ginnie's gifts, but it was hard to care about her new clothes and make-up, while all I wanted to do was burst into tears. My father watched quietly from his seat on the couch, then finally stood up and motioned for me to follow him.

"Come on outside, Bob. I have something I need to talk about with you." Slowly I got up off the floor, wondering what I had done. Putting my crutches under each arm, I walked across the room. Was I in trouble? Is that why there was nothing under the tree for me? As he led me out the front door and around the side of the house, I wracked my brain to figure out what it could be.

I was so lost in thought I almost tripped over the bright blue Honda 50 trail bike. Attached to the right side was a rectangular box — the sidecar the gentleman had rejected.

"Well, Bob, Merry Christmas!" My dad beamed, as pleased with my shock as with the gift itself.

"The sidecar! You put it on a bike for me? Really? The bike is mine?" I kept repeating, having a hard time believing my eyes.

"Yes, it's yours, son. I repaired it, and I think this provides the solution we were looking for. I rigged it so you can shift with your hand and don't need to use your foot. It will still tip over if you aren't careful, especially going around corners, but I think you will figure that out soon enough."

Stunned, I stood in the bright sunshine, staring at the answer to my dreams. I was going to ride my very own motorcycle. I walked all around it, touching the handlebars and seat, looking at the sidecar and how it was attached. Finally, I sat on the bike, pulling my right leg over the seat and resting my boot on the foot peg. Unlocking the knee brace so my other leg would bend, I lifted it up and placed my left foot on its peg. Realizing my crutches fit neatly in the open rectangular box of the sidecar, I shoved them in. The key was in the ignition.

My father explained the shifting mechanism. "I welded this long rod to the end of the foot shifter. You can see it comes straight up by your left handle bar, and I designed it so it doesn't interfere with steering. As you know, the Honda has a centrifugal clutch, so you don't need to worry about that, it works by itself." Making me practice shifting before letting me turn it on, he made sure I understood exactly how everything worked. Finally, I was ready.

"Okay, the driveway is long and straight. Drive down to the bottom, stop, turn it around and come back up," he pointed toward the packed dirt road that stretched almost a quarter mile toward the main street. "Take it slowly."

Everyone gathered on the porch to watch. Holding my breath, I started the engine, listening to the sound it made, taking it all in. This was really my bike; I was actually getting to drive. Making sure it was in first gear, I twisted the throttle and started moving.

"STOP, STOP!" the adults all screamed, although too late to prevent the crash. Ten seconds into driving and I had my first accident, hitting the wheel well of our friend's sedan parked on the side of the drive. They ran over to survey the damage. The fender of the sidecar was lying on the ground, and there was a nice scrape alongside the driver's door. I felt sick.

Please don't take it away! kept repeating in my head. "I'm sorry! I'm sorry!" was all that came out of my mouth.

"Not quite as easy as it looks, is it, son?" My father was smiling. I breathed a sigh of relief. He wasn't yelling; I wasn't in trouble; he wasn't going to take the bike. "You need to keep you eye on where you want to go. Don't look at the car off to the side, or you'll do what you just did, and keep hitting things. I'll pick up that fender off the ground and get it out of the way."

"It happens; we've all done it," our friend said. "Just start it up again and this time pay more attention to what you're doing."

Okay, here goes nothing, I said to myself. *I can do this*. Focusing my attention on steering it straight down the driveway, I started up again. Tentatively at first, gaining confidence with each pass of the house, I rode it up and down the road until it ran out of gas.

My world exploded. My previous experiences of independent movement had all been in water, where I was limited by the confines of a swimming pool. Now I was on land, and for the first time I felt like I could go anywhere. Being able to do something I wasn't 'supposed' to be allowed to do fit the view I had of myself, of someone who rebelled when told 'No, you can't.' Now I could ride alongside my father when he went camping with his friends. For the first time in my life I felt like a grown up.

My father and a group of his friends loved riding in the desert on the eastern side of the Sierras and I'd always tagged along. I loved being outside in the open air, sitting around the campfire at night, listening to their stories. Never lacking initiative, I explored as far as my crutches would take me. Climbing in and around the decrepit ruins in the old ghost town of Candelaria, Nevada, creating stories in my head of life in the days of the silver rush, I entertained myself while they were out riding. Now, finally, I watched as my bike was added to the others on the trailer, and climbed into the back seat of the truck to make the long trek across the mountains where I was going to ride as an equal.

I rode from sunup to sundown, only stopping long enough to beg the adults for spare gas whenever I ran out. I learned how to choose my routes, making sure the sidecar could navigate wherever I wanted to go.

"How was it going through that turn, Bob? Seems like you took a bit longer than the rest of us to get around."

I had nothing to compare the bike's handling with, and none of the adults were able to offer much in the way of instruction, never having ridden with a sidecar, either. Through trial and error I figured out how my bike worked, and sitting around the campfire in the evenings, I shared my growing knowledge with the others.

"Yes, it takes a bit longer to stop since there's more friction with three tires. It looks like I need a bit more room to turn than you do; the rig wants to keep going straight and I have to work to get it to turn, but once it starts the turn it's fine.

"I came close to tipping it over on one turn, but it actually took quite a bit of work to do that; it's got such a low center of gravity to help balance it." I felt quite grown up sharing my expertise.

I continued to ride only on dirt until I was fifteen and passed my driver's test, earning my learner's permit that allowed me to drive on public roads. My father and I modified the Honda for street use, and I wore through twenty sets of rings and pistons on that Honda, putting more than 100,000 miles on the odometer in just over three years.

For once, I was a typical teenager, driving anywhere, anytime, and any place.

My very own motorcycle, my first—a Honda 50
Tobie Stevens, photographer

1964

Only 121 cases of polio reported in the United States.

CHAPTER 8

When Henry Vande Graaf came to work for my father as the music teacher at the store, he took me under his wing. The church organist at his local parish, I accompanied him to Sunday services, and tagged along as he went to students' homes to teach lessons. He and his wife never had children, and welcomed me into their home as if I were their own. He was also a surrogate father to me, a role model of calm, and a strong, positive, influence in my life.

Henry started my formal tutelage in music. I had always made instruments as a young child, inventing contraptions with cardboard and strings, pretending to play as I watched my mother strum her guitar. My voice was strong and I had a natural aptitude for carrying a tune. Spending time alone, I composed songs and hummed melodies in my head, but I hadn't had lessons until Henry sat me down with the clarinet. I learned to play, although as I progressed I found I preferred the piano. Henry eventually taught me to play almost any instrument and my father shared his knowledge of tuning and repairing even the most damaged ones. My willingness to learn whatever they were willing to show me soon proved to them that I was a hard worker and a valuable asset at the store. My father asked me to begin teaching students when I was only fourteen.

School was still an exercise in futility. Kids teased me, making cruel remarks under their breath as I passed. I never knew anyone else who had polio, and from the reactions of my classmates it was clear they'd never known anyone with polio either. I was different from the other students both in my eyes and theirs. Unlike measles or other childhood diseases where symptoms flared and then disappeared, the stigma and fear of polio remained strong wherever I went. My body scared them, and my lack of social skills kept me from overcoming their revulsion. I wanted to fit in, and I tried hard at times. I even learned to lie about my body, denying I'd ever been sick.

"I was born this way." "I had an accident when I was a baby." The more I told these tales, made up stories about my crutches and braces, the more I found myself slowly disconnecting from my own experience of the disease. Anything was preferable to disclosing having had polio.

My legs may not have been strong, but my upper body was. I couldn't chase those who argued with me, but I could throw things and I had a mean swing. When my fist landed, it hurt. I was frequently in fights with other students.

"Where'd you get those black eyes?" my father called across the store. "Who'd you have it out with this time? I hope you gave as good as you got at least," the laughter in his voice confused me. Was he glad I was hurt or proud that I might have been tough enough to inflict equal harm to the other kid? With him, I never quite knew.

"It was over a girl," I admitted. "Apparently he likes her and didn't want me talking to her. It's not as if she liked me anyway." I shrugged, walking into the backroom to drop off my schoolbooks. "I just hope the swelling doesn't interfere with the oboe I need to work on today."

"Serves you right if it does," my father admonished. Henry, sitting in the corner watching our interaction, just chuckled.

~

Most of my fights occurred after school hours, but occasionally the provocation proved too much and I couldn't delay my anger.

"Okay, what did you do to start the fight?" The principal stared at me. "I have to believe you provoked him, Bob. I can't imagine he'd just throw the trash lid at you for no reason."

I stared back. "Why do you think I started it? Why can't it be his fault for once?" I implored. "You do know he knocked me out when it hit me; maybe I'm just sick of the way he treats me."

I didn't really expect the principal to listen; my experience over the years taught me it wasn't worth trying to convince anyone that the other kids were cruel. "What's the punishment this time?" I sighed, rubbing the lump on the side of my head.

"A three-day suspension; you for provoking it and his is for reacting with the lid. Now get out my office. I don't want to see either of you in here again," he said, standing up abruptly for emphasis.

~

School continued to be too easy for me. I devoured every book put in front of me, my memory was excellent, and I hated doing what to me was mindless work. With the exception of music classes, everything else felt like a waste of my time.

"If I get all A's on my tests, will you exempt me from homework?" I doubted my Algebra 2 teacher had received many such requests. "I read all the books the first month of school; they're just sitting in my locker. I already know this stuff."

He rubbed his chin, pondering the correct response. "If you get a single test score below a solid 'A' then the deal is off. If I find out you've told other students about this, same thing. I don't want a rebellion on my hands. Agreed?" he asked, looking directly at me. "One word to anyone and we're done."

"I can do that," I replied, relieved he bought my argument. I wondered if it would work with my other teachers. Surprisingly, most of them agreed.

My strategy worked beautifully until the following year. I was startled when my Biology teacher refused.

"No deals this year, Bob. You have to come to class, do the labs, and turn in your work."

"I don't understand. You let me do it last year in Algebra. Why the change?" I couldn't believe he would make me actually turn in daily work.

"Science is different, Bob. You have to be here, I need to observe you doing the labs and working with partners. This is a hands-on class; it's not a 'read and take a test' class. I want to see your lab write-ups. As I said, no deals."

"Fine. I don't like it, but apparently I don't have much choice, do I?" I walked out of the room frustrated I hadn't been able to make a dent in his argument. I showed up for class as he demanded, but refused to turn in the assignments weekly as required. On the last day of class I walked up to the front of the room and, pulling open my book bag, dumped a year's worth of homework papers and lab reports on his desk.

"You only said I had to turn in my work, you never specified when," my smug smile daring him to contradict me. Unable to refute my logic, he had no choice but to give me a passing grade.

~

"Bob, that's it, get out! I am tired of you disrupting class with your talking and clowning around," my World History teacher yelled at me across the room.

"Are you serious? I wasn't even talking! I was sitting here doing my work," I argued.

"Get out. I saw you; don't bother lying." He was adamant, which made me angry because it was one of the few times I wasn't actually guilty of the crime. I shoved my books into my book bag, slung it over my shoulder, grabbed my crutches, and left the room. Stopping in the hallway, I leaned against the lockers and reached into my satchel. I began rummaging around for something I vaguely remembered tossing in weeks before.

Ah, here it is. I pulled out the small cherry bomb leftover from the previous Fourth of July celebrations. *This ought to do the trick. Now, where are some matches?* I wanted retaliation for the embarrassment I had just suffered. I found an old match folder crumpled in the bottom of my bag. There were still a few left, just enough for my plan to work. I stuffed the matchbook and bomb in my pocket, picked up my things, and continued down the hallway to the boy's bathroom. Slipping inside unnoticed, I went into one of the stalls and closed the door. I placed the bomb on the edge of the toilet, tore a match from the book, and after two attempts striking it on the tiny strip of flint, it lit. Picking up the round ball of the bomb, I carefully held the flame to the fuse.

It caught. *Oh my god, what am I doing?* raced into my mind. Immediately regretting my decision, I tossed the lit bomb into the toilet, flushed it, and left the bathroom in a hurry.

"Kaboom!" I heard the explosion before I was halfway down the hall.

"An explosion. Everyone leave the building!" Shouts came from the floor below. "Get out now, it's an emergency!" As students and teachers poured out of the classrooms, I filed in beside them and we hurriedly made our way outside.

"What's happening?" I asked innocently, joining the hubbub of conversation as everyone tried to figure out what had caused the commotion.

"The wall in the principal's office blew open. A pipe in his bathroom exploded. The teachers are saying it might have been some kind of gas leak."

"Wow, that's scary!" I wanted to laugh, but I knew I had to keep a straight face. I certainly didn't want to arouse suspicion. I honestly had no idea the fuse would continue to burn under water as it travelled through the pipes that ran alongside the principal's office, but once it had, I took a moment to savor the power of my one small cherry bomb.

~

"Bob, you need to graduate. I know you hate school, but you'll be stuck in dead end jobs if you don't get that diploma." I was sitting in the empty classroom with Donald Whitehead, the Placer High School band director, after practice one day.

"You'll have enough credits if you stay in all your music classes and pass them. I'll work with the school to help minimize any other requirements you have left to complete. We just need to get you through your senior year." Mr. Whitehead was one of the few teachers whose opinion mattered to me.

"I don't mind taking music, but all the other stuff is garbage. I'm not learning, I hate the work, and I don't care about college. I have no idea what I'll do for a living, but it will be in music, so that's all that matters," I responded with the certainty of a seventeen-year-old.

"I know you believe you'll be fine, but I have more experience than you. You have to trust me on this one," he insisted. I did trust him, and if he really wanted to help me, I figured I could do my part.

"Anything to get out of this place," I reluctantly agreed.

He kept his word. And I kept mine, taking every music class offered, with the obvious exception of marching band. Playing the oboe in the orchestra and the symphony, clarinet in the jazz band, and singing in the various choirs kept me in school my final year. Mr. Whitehead ran interference for me with the teachers who wanted to hold me back, and my loyalty to him kept me going when my frustrations built to near exploding. My grades reflected my passions: garnering A's in every music class, and C's in everything else. Finally, thankfully, I graduated, and had to figure out my next steps.

I asked a young family friend whom I admired what path he had taken to become a musician. Taught piano tuning by my father, he worked at the store and I spent hours talking with him about music. Only four years older than me, I decided I wanted to follow in his footsteps.

"Where did you go to college? What did you like about it?" I asked him one afternoon while we were sitting in the store between customers.

"Azusa Pacific, just east of Los Angeles," he shared. "It's a great school with a strong music program. The students are friendly and the town is small, not too crowded. I'd be happy to write you a recommendation. It might help coming from an alumnus," he volunteered.

"My parents are pressuring me to go to college, and I have no idea where to apply, so thanks. I'll take you up on your offer." I was relieved to have at least one option available to me. I wrote to the college for the requisite application materials, dutifully filled out the paperwork, and submitted the necessary supporting documents. Looking at my transcript, I wasn't confident they'd take me. Miraculously, they not only accepted me despite my erratic high school record, they awarded me a scholarship in music. My mother was thrilled. A small Christian college, known for its rigid discipline and high moral standards, she believed it would give me one last chance to tame my rebellious ways.

~

Still driving the Honda, it made sense to take it with me when I left for college. It was cheap, reliable, and provided an easy form of transportation for any errands I might need to run. Packing the few belongings I needed for my dorm room, I headed to Azusa and began my next stage in life. I hoped that by focusing on music I might actually enjoy school. I also hoped that college students would show more maturity than those I had recently left behind, and was looking forward to a new start where no one knew me.

I was pleasantly surprised that my new classmates seemed more interested in my musical ability than the reasons for my crutches. I began making a few friends and quickly settled into a routine of classes, rehearsals, and practice.

Out one afternoon taking care of errands, I was returning to campus when a car suddenly turned left in front of me. "Oh shit!" I had no time to even grab the brakes. I heard the crunch of metal as my bike smashed into the passenger door, and I was suddenly airborne. Before I could even grasp what was happening, my head slammed on the asphalt and my body buckled underneath me. Pain radiated across my shoulder and down my arm. I couldn't move or catch my breath.

The driver slammed on his brakes, jumped out of the car, and raced over to me. "Are you okay, can you talk? Are you hurt?" he peppered me with questions.

It seemed like forever before the air rushed back into my lungs and I could breathe. As I slowly moved my head from side to side, I heard the crunch of gravel under my helmet and had a moment of gratitude that I had worn it that morning since I often left it sitting on the dresser in my room. Rolling onto my back, I took inventory. My hand was in pain. Everything else seemed to be sore, but okay. I slowly sat up. My fingers, twisted at odd angles, would need some attention, but even they didn't appear to be broken.

"My hand is messed up, my thumb and fingers are out of place, but I think I'm okay," I finally answered, hearing his sigh of relief as it sank in that my injuries were minor.

"I just need to gather my things and get back on my way," I continued. "But if you don't mind, could you grab those crutches out of the sidecar for me?"

He stopped and stared at me for a full minute, unsure how to respond.

"Holy shit, you certainly come prepared!" He shook his head before breaking into a laugh as he reached for my crutches.

The bike seemed to be fine, and I stood for a few minutes to make sure I really was okay. The man helped me gather my books that were strewn across the road and I piled them back into the sidecar.

"Glad you're going to be alright," he said as I nodded, climbed on the bike, and headed to the hospital to see about getting my hand examined. My fingers, as expected, needed straightening but the doctor told me once the swelling went down they'd be perfectly fine.

~

I liked girls in high school, but I'd never dated, saving myself the pain of rejection. College felt safer, the students more mature and accepting, and I finally gathered the courage to ask a classmate out. I was thrilled when she agreed to see *Gone With The Wind* with me at a local movie theater.

"Would you mind if we met in front of your place? I asked, slightly embarrassed. "My bike isn't designed to carry passengers, and I've never had anyone on the back with me. Would it be okay if we took your car?"

"Sure, that's fine. Shall we meet at six? I'm really looking forward to seeing the movie." I wasn't sure if she was as excited to see me, but I was happy I was finally going on a date.

The evening progressed nicely, and we chatted during the intermission. Emboldened by the ease of our conversation, I slipped my left arm around her shoulder. She didn't remove it, so I tried for a bit more. My hand made contact with a nice rounded part of her anatomy. Once again, she had no negative reaction. I was delighted, until I felt my arm slowly going to sleep. *What should I do? Do I dare move?* Ultimately, I decided it was worth any suffering to look cool.

The movie ended, and as the lights came on I looked over at her, smiling. I glanced briefly at her side. Oh my god, I'd been fondling her elbow! Mortified, I pretended that had been my intent all along. We gathered our things, and headed back to her apartment where we said a chaste goodnight. I never asked her out again.

~

"Bob, Henry died. No one expected it. We're all stunned." I was still in Southern California when the phone call came. I could hear the pain in my mother's voice. "You need to come home for the funeral." I was devastated. Henry, my mentor, second father, and friend, was gone.

The long ride to Sacramento gave me time to think. Grief stricken, fighting back tears, I focused on the road ahead, literally and metaphorically. The silence inside my helmet gave me the quiet I needed to evaluate my experience at Azusa Pacific. The music program at the college was excellent, and I had made friends, but I wasn't sure I fit in. I was becoming increasingly disillusioned with organized religion, and religion was the heart and soul of the college. I'd never become a believer despite the early exposure at various churches with my parents and my experience at Pine Hill Academy. I realized my growing cynicism was increasingly interfering with my education.

My thoughts continued to swirl as I listened to the speakers at Henry's funeral. I wasn't sure what to do or where to turn when Mrs. Vande Graaf approached me privately after the service.

"I need your help, Bob. Henry's students need a good teacher, and you know Henry had such faith in you. I was wondering if you'd consider taking over his work?" She was offering me a decent job with a ready-made clientele.

"I'd be honored. Henry did so much for me, it's the least I can do for him," I answered without hesitation. Henry cared deeply for his students; she didn't want just anybody taking his place. I could see the relief in her eyes. What she didn't see was the relief in mine. I had my answer. She'd just given me the excuse I needed to leave school. After only one year in Southern California, I returned home.

I transferred to Sierra Junior College in Auburn and began

pursuing music courses. Teaching music lessons filled part of my time, but I needed more income if I wanted to live on my own and not with my parents. A friend told me a local elementary school, Forest Hill, needed a band director, and despite my lack of degree, I applied. My credentials were advanced for my age, and I soon had a second job.

After completing all the courses available at Sierra, I transferred to Sacramento State College and moved into a commune nearby. My career path was starting to look like a patchwork of teaching, performing, piano tuning, and instrument repair. I met with the academic advisor.

"I don't really need more music classes. I've been doing music all my life. They're definitely the easiest for me, but I'm wondering if I should major in business. I see myself being self-employed and it might be helpful," I shared.

"You have enough credits for a minor in music already, so if you stack on a lot of business courses from now until you graduate, you'll fulfill the requirements of the major. And, I just noticed, if we just add a few extras, you'll be able to get your teaching credential as well. I think it's a very workable plan," he suggested. Together we mapped out the classes I would need.

Soon I was teaching at Forest Hill during the day, taking classes at Sac State at night, and fitting in private students in my spare hours. I was driving hundreds of miles a week on the Honda in between the different cities, rushing from one commitment to another with barely time to breathe. Commuting from school one afternoon, I was once again cut off by an inattentive driver.

"Dammit! Not again! I am sick of these stupid people!" Slamming on my brakes, I heard the tires squeal as the bike skidded several feet before coming to a lurching stop. I didn't move; I just sat on the seat, my hands on the handlebars. Slowly letting go of my death grip, I looked around for the other driver. All I saw was the rear end of the car, oblivious to the world, heading down the highway. Alone on the street, I sighed before restarting the bike and heading for home.

I am so done with this, I thought. *I'm tired of being run off the road, tired of being invisible, and tired of getting hurt. This isn't going to be the last time this is going to happen if I keep riding.* Thinking about the number of near misses I'd already had, I parked my bike in the garage, my riding days over. It was time to get a car.

I purchased a nearly new 1965 Plymouth Valiant for fifteen hundred dollars with a loan financed by my mother, and faced one minor problem: at nineteen I'd never needed to drive anything other than the Honda. Figuring it'd be easy to learn how to drive a car, I asked my father to teach me. The main challenge was figuring out what modifications I needed to accommodate my legs.

"I have an idea," I offered. "Let me sit there and see if it will work." My father climbed out of the driver's seat while I slid onto the bench seat, unlocking the left knee on my brace and lifting my leg into the car. "I've been watching you for awhile and trying to figure out how to get my leg to move between the gas and the brake. I have enough strength to use the pedals, I just don't have the lift to move from one to the other."

Using my right hand, I reached under my right leg and pulled it up, shoving it slightly to the left at the same time. I released it, dropping it squarely on the brake. Reversing the procedure, I maneuvered my foot back to the accelerator.

"I think this will work," I said, looking up at my dad for his reaction. "I'll need to practice, but I think I can do this pretty effortlessly once I get the hang of it. I can definitely feel the pedals and I can easily push up and down on them. I'm not worried about that at all," I continued, hoping he'd agree with my assessment.

"Not a bad system," he nodded. "You'll need to get faster. We'll need to go out on some empty roads so you can gain confidence, and so I can see that you'll be able to handle things in an emergency, but I like what you've come up with. Of course, you'll never be able to drive a stick shift with a clutch, but I don't see that as a problem."

After driving the car for three weeks, most of the time in the city commuting to my different jobs, I wanted to see how the Plymouth handled in less prescribed circumstances. Picking a drizzly Saturday morning for my test drive, I drove to a nearly deserted road on the outskirts of town.

"Now this could be fun," I laughed aloud. "Let's just open this baby up and give her a go." I pressed on the accelerator, surprised at the power. Used to my Honda, which could barely manage the speed limit on a good day, I was unprepared for the Valiant. Believing I should be able to drive as fast as the car's speedometer indicated it could go, I floored it.

I didn't factor in the rain. Coming into a corner, I realized a split second too late I was going too fast for the conditions. I felt the car sliding and tried to regain control before it hit the curb. Bouncing against it, the car spun and hit another curb before tipping on end.

'Oh shit, oh shit!' I screamed, slamming into the steering wheel before being whiplashed back against the seat as the car flipped end over end, finally coming to a stop against a telephone pole. Miraculously, the car was upright. My crutches had smacked me in the head as they flew through the air, but the small bruise on my forehead and the larger one on my right knee were all the damage I sustained. Unfortunately, the car wasn't as lucky. Climbing out to examine it, it was clear its driving days were over.

I continued to buy used, cheap cars. I ran through a 1959

Studebaker Lark, which I traded for a Scottish kilt when the engine died; a 1956 Mercury Montclair, dubbed 'The Mayflower,' telling friends, "If I can get a girl in it she'll come across;" and an Oldsmobile Cutlass in addition to several others along the way. None lasted long since it was usually cheaper to get a new one than repair the old one.

~

The wear and tear of juggling school and work finally caught up with me. One day, after falling asleep in class yet again, I realized I had reached my limit. Stopping by my parents' house that evening for dinner, I broached the topic of school.

"I don't think I want to keep doing this," I shared. "I'm exhausted, and I'm not sure it's worth it just for a degree. I already have all I need for the teaching credential, and I don't see a reason to finish one last semester just to say I did it."

"Your life, your decision," was my father's only response. "I never went to college and I've been successful. The important thing is that you can earn a living."

I wasn't seeking their approval, but it was nice to know I had it. The next morning, I drove to campus and withdrew.

We were always playing music at home (circa 1959)

Pop and Henry Vande Graaf,
who was like a second father to me (1959)

CHAPTER 9

After dropping off some papers at a friend's house, I walked outside and looked around for my car. *It was right here; where the hell did it go?* It took a minute for me to comprehend it had been stolen. I called the police to report it missing and worried about my dog, who had been sitting quietly inside when I'd gone upstairs. The next day I walked through the run-down neighborhood, hoping to find both the car and the culprit, figuring whoever had taken it intended to use it himself. Turning a corner into a small, nearly deserted alleyway, I spied the car. The thief was sitting in the front seat, his head leaned back with the window rolled down, smoking a cigarette. He didn't see me. I snuck up behind him, grabbed open the driver's door, and yanked him out of the car, shoving him to the ground. I jumped on him, my rage taking over all my senses.

"Why'd you take my car?" I screamed. "And where's my dog, you sonofabitch!"

"Dead," he answered, without a trace of remorse. "I needed a car and he was in my way. Whatcha gonna do about it?" He tried to shove me off, assuming I'd be an easy mark. I lost all remaining control.

"You bastard! You sonofabitch!" The words poured out of my mouth as fast as my fists were beating him. Sitting on top of him, I pounded him, striking his head, his chest, anywhere I could land a blow. I smashed his head against the concrete, then finally stopped, exhausted and depleted. Blood seeped out from the cuts around his face and his eyes were already starting to swell. Grabbing the crutches I'd flung down in my rage, I stood up and took one last look at him lying on the asphalt.

"That's what I'm gonna do about it," I spit at him. I turned and walked away. Locating a pay phone at a nearby gas station, I called the police to report both the sighting of the car and an injured man in the street. I never identified myself as either the owner or the assailant.

Shaking, I went home and sat for a long time contemplating the events of the past hours. My hands were bruised and scraped. The death of my dog, an innocent bystander, was devastating. I tried to justify my actions. I always had a temper, but I had always been able to control it. The depth of my rage scared me.

Exhausted, I went into the bathroom to wash my face. Standing in front of the mirror, my eyes red and swollen, I stared at my reflection. My father's face stared back at me, and it terrified me.

"You're no different than me, son," his voice echoed in my ears. "You've always thought you were better, but see, you're just like me." Witnessing his explosiveness throughout my childhood, all too often watching him shove my mother out of his way or slamming her against a wall, I had vowed to contain my anger, and now I had failed. I had done the same thing; was I really like him? Because my anger had always been directed at an adversary rather than someone I loved, I'd always been able to justify my actions. But if I could lose control like that, maybe I, too, was capable of rage if a partner made me mad. I felt as though I was seeing myself for the first time, and I didn't like the image in front of me. Talking aloud, I soon found myself yelling at my reflection.

"You are heading nowhere!

"You're hurting people and wasting your talents!

"You're angry at the world for only seeing your polio, not you, but it's up to you to change that!"

I felt tears welling up. My anger was destroying me; it wasn't who I wanted to be or how I wanted to feel. I slid to the floor and cried, the wracking of my sobs reverberating in the small room. I felt something inside me release as a wall of loneliness and hurt I had lived with all my life broke down, replaced by a sense of calm and focus. I could hear faint strains of Henry's voice in my ear, his belief in me supplanting the despair I had felt only moments before.

"Think about what you want to do with your life. You are smart and capable, and it's time to own that. If you want people to see you as a person, you need to be a person worth looking at.

"What will take you where you want to go? What will make you a better person? Set goals, make a difference.

"Learn the skills you need to be comfortable in any situation. Walk into a room and own it.

"Be a success. You have value; now go out there, goddammit, and do something with your life!"

1968

Salk's inactivated vaccine phased out as Sabin's attenuated vaccine becomes the gold standard across the United States.

CHAPTER 10

I stood in front of my bathroom mirror every morning, making faces and trying to figure out what different expressions meant. What was a friendly smile, what was a smirk? I noticed how hard it was to look myself in the eye, so I forced myself to spend hours becoming comfortable with direct contact. I started telling stories, noticing my reactions to what I was saying and how I was saying it. I even sang to my reflection. I felt silly at first, self conscious and awkward. How stupid was I that I needed to practice such simple skills that others seemed to take for granted.

One night, laughing at one of my own jokes, it hit me; I'd spent my early developmental years in the hospital interacting with very few people, all with masks covering much of their faces. One-on-one interactions often focused on, 'Bobby, I'm going to stretch your leg' or 'Bobby, I know this hurts but it's for your own good to help you get better.' The nurses and doctors didn't have time to sit and play games, read to me, or ask about my day. I spent hours staring at the ceiling, lost in books, or conversing with myself in my head. I'd never learned the subtleties of social interaction. Because of the irrational fears and prejudices of school administrators, my elementary education was almost exclusively at home, a crucial time when kids learn to make friends and resolve conflicts on the playground. I'd never had sleepovers or been invited to birthday parties. Attending middle and high school had only reinforced my awkwardness, as students teased or shunned me. Left to my own devices I hadn't practiced the skills of negotiation, listening, or caring. Fighting with my sister primarily focused on how to best her at everything, not how to get along. Teaching students hadn't required me to understand them emotionally; I simply needed to make sure they knew how to play the instrument in front of them. I had made some friends as I got older, but really hadn't yet learned how to be one.

I practiced my newfound skills with everyone I met. Deliberately engaging in conversations, I watched for the reactions of others and learned to modify my actions in response. My ability to read faces and expressions improved and I noticed my circle of friends slowly growing. My awkwardness around others slowly diminished, and I began looking forward to my interactions with people rather than merely tolerating them.

Mature-looking for my age, I often had gigs singing and playing in bars even though I was still under twenty-one. Pleased with my progress with casual friendships, I now wanted to extend my comfort to relationships with women. I began looking for opportunities to talk to them while on breaks at work, and learned to engage in small talk. I found I actually enjoyed listening when they shared their stories.

Despite my growing confidence, I knew was too young to get involved in any serious relationships, and the thought of getting married terrified me. I wanted to date, and even be monogamous, but I certainly didn't want to commit for the rest of my life. My experience in the bars led me to the conclusion that the younger a woman was, the more focused she seemed to be on marriage. Women a bit older than me seemed to be more intent on having fun and were content to allow a relationship take its course without an end result. If I wanted to have a good time and avoid hurting someone who was in search of a long-term commitment, I needed to narrow my attention to those older women.

Scrupulously honest, making my intentions clear from the start, my suppositions were confirmed; I found surprisingly little resistance to my lack of interest in marriage. Dating quickly emerged as my favorite recreational pursuit, with learning to play poker a distant second. Music was my passport. Singing, playing guitar, and the piano made me cool, and no one cared about my legs as long as the rest of me worked fine, and thankfully, it did.

My plan to remain single was working perfectly until a friend and I went out to have a few drinks one evening after work. Ten years older than me, she had been incredibly supportive when my car was stolen and my dog killed. I never was one to over indulge in booze, and I never touched drugs, but that night — chatting, laughing, and flirting — we both had a few too many.

"The only thing I've never experienced is getting married," she tossed out lightly. "How 'bout we flip a coin. Heads, we go find a justice of the peace, tails we go home."

"Doesn't matter to me, don't care either way," I answered, believing in my hazy stupor we were simply sharing a good joke.

"Heads. Looks like we're getting married." We both laughed.

I called my folks to let them know we were heading to Reno, where we spent three days in a hotel before sobering up and returning to reality.

Well, shoot, what the hell just happened? Those papers on the table seem legit. This marriage looks like the real deal. Damn, I guess I've got to get serious now, I thought. This new twist wasn't at all in the plans, but I wanted to be a man of my word. Neither of us knew quite what to do, and neither of us knew how to broach the subject of what we'd just done. So, without any real discussion, we headed back to Sacramento and started looking for a place to live. After we signed papers for a run-down rental house, she took off to Modesto to 'get some things.' Thankfully for both of us, she never returned. The marriage was quickly, and mutually, annulled.

I contemplated my next steps. Looking for a clean break, and wanting to avoid the judgmental looks from my parents, on a whim I decided to follow one of the families I taught, moving with them to Idaho Falls, Idaho. Other than their five children as students, I had no income. The town was small and jobs were scarce. Convincing a local pizza parlor owner to hire me as entertainment to supplement my teaching income was challenging.

"If customers increase, keep me on. If they don't, I'm out of here, no skin off your back, no obligation. You can't lose, and I know I can do it," I said in my most confident voice. If he didn't hire me, I wasn't sure how I would make ends meet.

"Fine, I'll give you one month. Let's see what you can do. You can start tonight," he agreed. "But you'll need to pitch in around here as well. You can help in the kitchen and pour beers in between your sets. In exchange you can have one meal a day; no free loading." It sounded perfect; at least I wouldn't starve.

Spending most of my evenings at the pizza parlor and partying with others I'd met during my off hours, I was in love with my life. I was bringing in a lot of business, the owner was happy, and I was making enough money not only to support myself but to put some into savings. For the first time I had a large group of friends, and women flocked around me.

"Hey, Bob, what happened to your legs? Why do you use crutches?" friends often queried.

"Skiing accident in high school.

"Too fast around a corner with the car; totaled it and me!

"Motorcycling accident, guy cut me off. It was ugly!"

Although polio no longer threatened the public, I continued to live with the stigma from my childhood. No one knew my past, and whenever asked, I made up stories; anything was preferable to admitting I had polio. I was a master at changing the subject.

"Hey, have you heard this new song? I just figured out the music to it. Listen!" I wasn't about to engage in conversations where I might arouse either aversion or sympathy.

One night, two young women came in and one of them caught my eye. I invited her to sit with me while I played, and slowly a comfortable friendship developed. Stopping by every evening, she shared her stories after finishing my gig. I enjoyed her company and felt empathy for her tales of poverty and her desire to go somewhere with her life. An overwhelming urge to help arose in me, and flush with money, I offered my assistance.

"Betty, let me help put you through school. I know your family doesn't have the money to pay for it. I want to see you make something of yourself," I implored.

"Thanks for your generosity, but I'd rather get my MRS," she teased. "My family wouldn't approve of me taking money from someone, and my mother's been on my case to get married. You know how it is with Mormons! Even though I'm not practicing, my family still is and it's been instilled in me since I was a kid. Marry me, then I'll feel more comfortable taking your money," she laughed.

"Well, okay, if that's what you want, let's get married then," I replied, chortling as I joined in the joking. "Sure, I'm just dying to get married instead of giving you a loan!"

"Really? Did you just propose? Well, then, I accept!" She reached over and hugged me. Still chuckling, I waited for her to come back with "Just kidding!"

"Oh, this is wonderful! You're such a good friend and listener, and now you're going to be my husband!" In a sudden, horrible instant I realized she hadn't been teasing. She thought my proposal was serious, and she had just accepted it.

No! I wanted to scream out loud. *I only said it in jest!* But all I could manage was a weak smile. In an instant, she jumped up, yelling across the entire bar, "Bob just proposed! We're going to get married!"

I wanted to help her, but I never dreamed she'd been serious. I had no desire to get married, but I was suddenly trapped. She had just announced it to the world, and would be humiliated if I disillusioned her in front of her friends. I cared about her enough to want to spare her that embarrassment, and besides, how bad could it be? I liked her; she was a good friend. Maybe it was time for me to step up and be a man.

The next few days were a whirlwind. Before I had a chance to change my mind, our parents came to town, licenses were obtained, and a ceremony was planned. Standing in front of the officiant of the Rigby Mormon Church, this time I was totally sober and aware of what I was saying.

"Robert, do you take..." the words he spoke made no real sense to me. I hadn't converted nor did I intend to, but the officiant's cheery voice buoyed my spirits. Perhaps this was another step on my path toward wholeness, and it was a sign of maturity for me to accept this challenge.

"I do," I pledged, hoping I was doing the right thing. "I do."

~

Within the first two weeks I knew we'd made a dreadful mistake. Neither one of us was ready for marriage. Despite her conversations about attending college to get a degree, Betty had no intention of enrolling. I didn't want to be a husband, coming home every night, no longer free to do what I wanted. My lack of relationship skills combined with her indirectness contributed to the tension. Our arguments, infrequent at first, soon escalated into screaming fights with Betty taking off, slamming the door as she left. Then, as our tempers cooled, we reconnected, the physical attraction overriding our anger.

Our relationship began to feel like an addiction; I hated our fighting, but once I calmed down I missed her and experienced increasing anxiety until she returned, sometimes hours, and occasionally days, later. Unfortunately, our reconciliations didn't last long. Still, I was too blinded by my emotions in the early years to consider leaving, and besides, I felt honor bound to keep my promise. I'd already annulled one marriage, and was mortified at the thought annulling a second one.

"Maybe things will be better back in California. This cold is getting to me. I'm really a warm weather guy." Sitting around the breakfast table one morning after a particularly pleasant evening together, I was hopeful a change in location would help our marriage. Work in Idaho was starting to slow down, and I was ready to go home. "I've wanted to get into the piano tuning, restoration and repair business, and it's definitely a better market down there. I have a lot of contacts, and I can always take on music students."

"I don't really care where we live, and I'm sick of the cold as well. Warm sounds good to me." Betty was agreeable. I quit my job at the pizza parlor, we loaded up our few belongings, and headed south. Settling in Rancho Cordova, about thirty miles from my parents, I set up shop, reaching out to former clients and establishing new ones. To make ends meet while building my

119

business, I started teaching at Bud and Helen Seward's Cordova Music Center and performing at local bars. I was soon working sixteen to eighteen hour days, falling into bed exhausted every night. Our fighting was less, but only because I was never home. When I did come around, she constantly brought up starting a family.

"Look, you knew I came from a Mormon family when you married me. You knew kids were important to me. I don't understand why you are fighting me on this." Betty was relentless.

"And you knew I didn't want children. I'm not good with kids, I don't have any time for kids, I don't have any desire to start a family!" I was equally adamant. "I work hard enough to take care of the two of us. I don't want to add to that pressure. I repeat: I do not want children!"

Our arguments were endless. As long as Betty was using birth control I felt our marriage still had a chance. Bringing kids into it seemed like a recipe for disaster.

~

"I'm pregnant!" Betty gleefully announced one afternoon. "The doctor says everything looks great."

"You're what?" I stared at her, unable to comprehend the words coming out of her mouth. "You're pregnant? How in the world did you get pregnant? You've been using protection!"

"Oh, I stopped that awhile ago. I told you I wanted children, so I quit using anything. Can't get pregnant any other way!" She giggled, pleased with herself.

Stunned, I stood up and left the house, in that moment not sure if I'd ever return.

Just great. You're already in a marriage you can't stand; now you're going to have a kid you don't want. My head was pounding as I drove around aimlessly. *You're so damn honorable; now see where it's gotten you.* I knew I was miserable, but I also knew I wasn't going to leave. I'd made a promise, and now I was stuck with it.

Sonja was born with medical complications. Despite my anger at Betty, I fell in love with my daughter, and it was painful to watch some of her early struggles. I spent hours clearing her nasal passages to help her breathe. Betty took her to her frequent medical appointments, and we took turns rocking her gently when she fussed. She was somewhat delayed in walking and her speech was difficult to understand, but we had no other children with whom to compare. To me she was perfect.

When she was born, I had a brief moment of hopefulness that our daughter would bring us closer together. But as had been our pattern, Betty and I argued about every aspect of parenting, disagreeing about discipline and routines; whatever the issue, it seemed we ended up on opposite sides.

~

"Mr. Mutchler, there's been an accident. Your wife and daughter are going to be fine, but you need to come down here and pick them up," the nurse's voice was calm and reassuring. "They're here in the Emergency Room. The receptionist will direct you when you get here."

At the hospital, I promptly found Betty and Sonja. Other than being rattled by the experience, they both seemed to be unharmed. Betty filled me in on the accident while we waited for the doctor to return with the discharge papers.

"We were out running errands when some idiot pulled out of the side road and hit us. Luckily, he wasn't going that fast or it could have been a lot worse. The doctor says he wants to chat with both of us now that you're here."

I reached over to pick up Sonja and was holding her as he came into the room.

"Everyone's going to be fine. Mostly bruises and some sore muscles, nothing worse," he informed me, taking a seat next to me. "So, how have the two of you coped with Sonja's developmental delays?"

"What are you talking about, Doc?" I asked. I had no idea what he meant. "You just said everyone was fine."

"Well, everything is fine as far as the accident. I meant Sonja. It's clear she has Down's syndrome. I was just wondering how well she is doing; how your family is dealing with her?"

Betty and I both stared at him. Sonja was barely three. Our family doctor had never said anything to either of us about anything being wrong with her, always focusing on whatever ailment we had taken her in for.

"Sonja is just fine. We honestly don't know what you are talking about. She may be a bit slower learning some things than other kids, but that's because of her health issues. We know she has some speech delays, but we're working with her and we're confident she'll be speaking soon. She isn't retarded; she's barely three-years-old! It takes some kids longer than others. She's just fine!"

Protectively bundling her up, I stood up. "I think we're done here. Even if what you are saying is true, it doesn't change anything." Handing her to Betty, we carried Sonja out to the car and sat her on the seat. Betty and I looked at each other.

"It doesn't matter what he thinks, or what he says. She's still our little girl, and we're going to raise her as normally as we can," I insisted, remembering how my parents had raised me. For once, we agreed. I started the car and headed home.

Our harmony was short-lived, resulting in another unplanned pregnancy and a resumption of our pattern of fighting followed by avoidance of each other. Our second daughter, Robyn, was born a year later, and Sonja had open-heart surgery shortly after to correct a congenital defect, common among children with Down syndrome. Despite loving my daughters, nothing had changed, and I now felt completely trapped.

1970

Abnormal fatigue, difficulty concentrating, sudden attacks of
sleepiness, in addition to muscle weakness and sensitivity to cold,
especially in the extremities,
are reported in a paper by three British lung specialists.

1974

The World Health Assembly creates the Expanded Program on
Immunization to target providing vaccines worldwide.

1970-80

Noting widespread polio outbreaks in many developing countries,
routine immunization with oral polio vaccine is included in
almost all national immunization programs.

CHAPTER 11

"Bob, I'd like you to come to lunch with me at Rotary today," said Bud Seaward, owner of the music store. His friendly tone hid the very clear implication that my attendance wasn't optional. New to the job, I was dependent upon his goodwill.

"Of course, I'd love to." I had no idea what Rotary was, but assumed it was just a quick one-time event, so I followed his friendly 'suggestion' and attended my first meeting.

Driving to the Cordova Lodge together, I followed Bud down the hallway to the banquet hall set aside for the group. When I entered the large room, I noticed I was the youngest person in the assembly by at least half. Men stood around chatting while someone played a piano in the background. The only women I observed were the staff from the hotel, waitresses bringing in drinks and setting up lunch.

(It wasn't until 1987 that women were allowed to join, following a Supreme Court decision ruling that charity clubs primarily used for business purposes and which often include non-members at their meetings must admit women. Officially changing their policy in 1989, Rotary saw a dramatic increase in participation by women as well as a continued trend of growth overall.)

Bud walked me around the room, introducing me to his friends and business acquaintances. Smiles and handshakes greeted me, making me feel very welcome despite the obvious age differences. My background as an entertainer helped overcome any awkwardness I might have felt.

"Bud mentioned you play the piano and sing. Would you mind playing a few songs for us?" The invitation was generously extended at the conclusion of the luncheon meeting. "We love a good sing-a-long."

"Sure. I think I can play some tunes you might know." I smiled and sat down at the bench, playing a few notes to warm up. The men gathered around the piano, and were soon singing in a harmonious chorus.

"That was delightful, Bob. We'd love to have you come again and play for us." The invitation was heartfelt. I realized I wanted to return to this group, not only to perform, but also to learn more about their mission and to partake in the camaraderie of this congenial group of men. It wasn't long before I found myself in the role of honorary member and piano player for their weekly gatherings.

Finding friendships within the group and learning more about Rotary's non-political and non-religious stances, my interest in joining was piqued. Originally started in 1905 by Paul Harris as a social and networking group for professionals, Rotary International rapidly evolved into a community service organization. The name, Rotary, was derived from the early practice of rotating meeting sites between different office locations.

I learned that members volunteered their time in numerous activities. I discovered the organization did more charitable work than almost any other group, which appealed to me after my earlier experiences with formal religion. A separate entity within Rotary,

The Rotary Foundation, was created in 1928, and in 1930 the foundation's first grant of $500 was given to the International Society for Crippled Children, an organization started by a fellow Rotarian that in 1967 changed its name to the more familiar Easter Seals. The Rotary Foundation has raised over $1 billion dollars since its inception in 1927, and the monies focus on six major areas: peace and conflict resolution; water and sanitation; maternal and child health; education and literacy; economic and community development; and disease prevention and treatment.

Everything I was learning about Rotary continued to impress me. But if I was going to keep attending, I wanted to be a full member, with voting privileges and a say in what was happening. I wanted to offer my services as more than the piano player; I wanted to contribute to the myriad of works both locally and globally in which Rotary partook.

Sponsorship by a current member of Rotary is necessary to be initiated into a club, as is a requirement to either be in upper management or a business owner. For some reason, Bud Seaward wasn't very encouraging of my desire to join, perhaps simply content to let me remain an honorary member, useful for my talents but not quite up to his image of an ideal Rotarian. Well, if he or the others weren't interested in me, then I'd have to look elsewhere. But I wasn't ready to give up that easily.

One of my new friends, local doctor Merlin Mauk, obviously had more belief in my abilities as an upstanding citizen. Chatting with him about my desire to join, he offered to endorse me for membership without a moment's hesitation, and I was thrilled when I was inducted into the group as a full participant.

My life soon settled into a comfortable routine. Work kept me busy. I was tuning pianos, repairing instruments, and teaching music during the day, while playing as many gigs at night as I could line up. Seeking out Rotary meetings, I quickly learned when groups met, joining them for lunches most days. Free weekends I often took the girls fishing and camping or participated in Sonja's Special Olympics activities. Rarely home with Betty, I found a way to avoid my marriage while remaining a respectable father and provider.

~

"What? What is it? Where am I?" Awaking with a jolt, it took me several minutes to orient myself. I shook my head to clear my mind, and looked around. I was in the shop, slouched over my workbench, the overhead lights still blazing. I glanced at the clock: 3 a.m.

"What the hell? How did this happen?" My voice echoed in the empty room. My head hurt, and reaching up to rub it, I felt a lump where I'd apparently fallen on the saxophone I'd been repairing. I must have passed out. *This is insane. What am I doing here in the middle of the night?* Burning the candle at both ends, I didn't notice I was driving myself into exhaustion. I had been going nonstop for months and it finally caught up with me.

I sat back in my chair. I couldn't keep doing this. I couldn't keep running myself into the ground, beating myself up like I'd been. I'd been focused on making my business a success, worrying about money, not only making ends meet but trying to become well-off in the process. I'd been taking work whenever it came my way no matter how busy I was already, figuring one more job meant much more in the bank at the end of the month.

I was successfully avoiding my marriage with my insane schedule, but I was miserable anyway. This was no way to live. The realization that I was killing myself hit me hard. I could either die rich and young, or I could be happy and have a life. Given that choice, it was obvious I had to make some changes, and I had to

128

make them now.

"We need to simplify things. One way is to reduce our living costs," I shared with Betty. "Rancho Cordova is a lovely place, but it's expensive to live here. I think we can find cheaper housing if we go further east. They've been building a lot of tract homes around the Folsom area, and I bet we can find something out there."

Discussions between us were rare by this point. I wasn't really asking Betty for her opinion, I was simply letting her know my plans.

"I'm going to go on Saturday and start looking if you want to drive out there with me." I didn't expect her to come.

"You go look and I'll stay with Sonja and Robyn. When you find something you like, let me know. If I hate it I'll tell you, otherwise I don't really care where we live as long as there are decent schools for the girls." Surprised by her sudden cooperativeness, and silently relieved she wasn't interested in spending the day together, I ended the conversation on that positive note.

I found a great little house in Folsom. It was in lousy condition, so the price was a steal. I thought I could bring it up to a decent standard with the help of the neighbor I met. Since it had been in such a state of disrepair for so long, he was excited to have someone interested in buying it. The lot was huge; walking around the property I could easily envision building a shop in the back with a storage space upstairs, and still have plenty of room for the girls to have a nice backyard to play in.

Betty visited the schools to see how they could work with Sonja, wanting to make sure she would be in a good, supportive learning environment. Betty had always handled her education and it was important to both of us that she continue making the progress she had shown so far.

Within weeks the papers were signed, initial repairs to the house completed, and work had begun on the new two-story building that would house my repair shop. Rather than a storage room I had originally imagined, I designed a living space on the second floor, and without any further discussion, I moved into the apartment upstairs. Betty and I were now living separately, an acknowledgement of the state of our marriage.

I transferred to the Folsom chapter of Rotary, and before long, made new friends. From chapter board positions to district office roles, I chaired various committees and volunteered for numerous activities. Trying to limit my hours to prevent the weariness that prompted the move, I spent my spare time with the girls while still avoiding Betty and any discussions regarding our deteriorating marriage.

"Bob, I'm going to England next week. I don't know how long I'll be gone or when I'll be back. I'm leaving the girls with you."

Despite the total disconnect in our relations, Betty's announcement still came as a surprise.

"I need time to sort things out and I don't want to deal with you while I'm thinking things through." The finality of her statement told me there was no changing her mind even if I had wanted to.

"Fine. Have a good trip." All I felt was relief.

When she returned six months later it was clear neither of us wanted to make any attempts at repairing our marriage. We mutually arrived at the decision to divorce, and finally, that chapter of my life came to a close. Betty moved out into her own house nearby, and Sonja chose to move with her mother while Robyn opted to remain with me. Self-employment gave me the flexibility to remain a single parent, able to help her get off for school most mornings and home in time to make dinner. When I played gigs late at night, she was old enough to be left alone—with our neighbor on standby in case of an emergency. Sonja visited on weekends and the three of us still took our camping trips together. I no longer felt the need to avoid home, and life settled into a quiet, comfortable routine.

1979

The last documented naturally occurring cases of polio in the
United States occur in the Amish communities
in several Midwestern states.

1980

A group of Italian doctors report that late-onset problems in polio
survivors are no longer a rare occurrence, and that it is a syndrome
different from the original disease.

1981

First post-polio syndrome conference commences, leading to the
recognition of Post Polio Syndrome as a specific diagnosis.

CHAPTER 12

"I don't get it. I can't seem to stay focused for more than a few minutes. My body aches all over." Chatting with Merlin, who had become my personal physician, over lunch one day, I bemoaned my increasing lack of energy.

"It used to take me ten minutes to get dressed, and now it takes a lot longer. I'm struggling to pull myself upright when I'm in bed; I have to use my right leg for leverage. The last time I remember having to do that was when I was little and just out of the hospital. I'm only thirty-six; I'm too young to be feeling this old!"

The fatigue had come on slowly, and at first it was easy to dismiss. Making it through the day had never been an issue before, but it was becoming more and more apparent that I was struggling and something unusual was happening with my body and my energy. I was taking naps after lunch and nodding off when I sat down to read a book after dinner. What was going on?

"The pain is excruciating. It hasn't been this bad since I was a kid. It hurts from the moment I wake up and doesn't let up all day. My joints, my muscles; everything feels like it's on fire. I can't get comfortable. I'm exhausted but I keep waking up all night.

"And the other day, getting up from my chair, I lost my balance and fell. This is not normal; something is definitely wrong. I'm starting to wonder if I had a stroke."

I'd been ignoring my symptoms, thinking I had once again taken on too much. At first attributing my listlessness to the divorce and single parenting for the past several months, I had to finally admit out loud that what I was experiencing wasn't a passing issue.

Merlin encouraged me to make an appointment with a neurologist. At first I demurred, convincing myself a different doctor wouldn't be of any help, but he persisted and I finally set up a meeting.

Sitting in the specialist's office following the exam, I tried, once again, to rationalize away my symptoms.

"I'm fine, just need to get a bit more sleep is all.

"I've been going through a lot with the divorce, that bad car accident last year, and taking care of the girls by myself, that's it.

"Even in the worst scenario, if it was a stroke, I'm doing fine; whatever damage it may have done is done. I'm okay, all things considered." My words hung in the air of the examining room. Was I trying to convince the doctor or myself?

"I'm 99 percent sure you didn't have a stroke. I believe it's the polio that's at the root of this, and not you working too much," he said quietly. "I've been reading up on what they are calling 'Post Polio Syndrome' and your symptoms fit the literature. Let's have you looked at by another doctor; I'd like to get a second opinion although I'm fairly certain his answer will be the same."

Thunderstruck by his words, I shut down. There was no way I had polio, post polio, or anything to do with polio. The neurologist continued rambling, his voice fading into a blur as I pulled myself up from the chair. I was convinced a different doctor would concur it was simply exhaustion.

"Yes, it's Post Polio syndrome all right, and the prognosis isn't good," the second neurologist said, confirming what the first one had feared. "You've got one, maybe two years and then you'll most likely end up in a wheelchair. I've seen it before with folks who had polio as children. It's not polio again; we think your body's worn out from the damage done when you were a kid. Your remaining nerves are giving up; the work they had to do to compensate for the ones destroyed by the virus has taken its toll. There's nothing we can do except help you prepare for it."

Furious, I left his office. Over the next few months, desperate to find a doctor who would clearly see the others had made a mistake, I made appointment after appointment, only to be given similar dire predictions. Researching on my own, I found little encouragement. Most stories told of a gradual decline; after recovering from childhood polio, people who led active lives saw their symptoms emerge again as they grew older.

In a wheelchair.

Unable to stand unassisted.

Bedridden.

In an iron lung.

Their words echoed endlessly in my head, crushing me. I felt lost. I'd driven myself to exhaustion trying to achieve something, and now my body was betraying me. I'd been able to fight my way in life, never giving into the "I can't" mentality; was it all for nothing? According to everything I read, I was going to end up in a wheelchair anyway. In my mind, that meant the polio had won.

Withdrawing from everything and everyone, I came out of my

135

hibernation only long enough to work to make ends meet. I took an open-ended sabbatical from Rotary, distancing myself from the friendships I had formed over the years. I didn't want anyone's pity and I didn't want anyone's opinions as to what treatments I should pursue. For the first time in my life I wasn't sure where to turn or what to do.

All I felt like doing was to stay in bed, pull the covers over my face, and disappear. And for days on end, that's often what I did. I wallowed in self-pity, replaying all the negative thoughts I'd kept at bay. Focusing on the positive had helped me make something of myself, but now I struggled to find the good in me, or in any of my accomplishments. All I saw was a loser, and all I wanted to do was give up.

Betty had constantly told me I was an evil person, always accusing me of selfishness. Was there truth in her assessment of me? I'd learned to control my temper, I'd made positive contributions as a father, but did I have blind spots? Was I focusing only on my good qualities and ignoring the bad? Arguments ping-ponged inside my head, debating what kind of life I'd led, and where I was heading. Once again, while getting ready in the mornings I often found myself talking aloud in front of the mirror.

"Who am I? What's good about me? What's bad about me? Was Betty right? Am I selfish?

"Yes; I often act selfishly when it suits me." I didn't like hearing that answer, yet I recognized the truth in the statement. I jumped immediately to defending my actions.

"I'm driven to achieve; I want to make something for my family and myself. It's a good thing, not selfish.

"But my actions often hurt others. Sometimes I am just doing what I want to do and justifying it later." It hurt to say it aloud. I didn't like seeing myself as a jerk.

"What's behind this? Is it really just wanting to be a success, to make a decent life?"

I was conflicted. Part of me was driven to achieve, to make something of myself, to prove I was as good as anyone else. What was driving that need? Who was I trying to impress, and why?

As I dug deeper, I also came to see that while I was never consciously aware of resenting my polio, the reality was I had lived much of my life denying I'd ever had it despite the obvious outward permanent effects. The pain of being different was still there, and I recognized it was that part of me I hated. I'd conditioned myself to believe I was infallible, that I could overcome anything, that by not admitting I was different I wouldn't be. The Post Polio diagnosis was slapping me in the face, forcing me to confront a reality I had avoided for years.

I took a deep breath and looked at my body; for the first time, really seeing myself. I'd become so efficient at getting myself into my braces, into my clothes, and out of the door that I hadn't connected to my physical self. Sitting on the side of my bed, I rubbed my hand down my left leg, feeling my skin under my fingertips. I noticed the difference in size from one leg to the other. The flaccid muscles on the left, shorter by inches than the right, were unable to keep my leg from falling uselessly to the side. The much stronger right, used to propel me forward and balance me when standing, was still unable to keep my foot from flopping down without a brace. My spine, curved from scoliosis and years of leaning against my crutches, was severely twisted, causing pain if I sat for long periods. My well-developed upper body, exercised throughout my life, was also a source of discomfort from years of overuse.

I'd never known any other way of being. I'd thought that I had accepted my body. Now I realized I had simply disconnected from it, mistaking avoidance for strength. True strength came from confronting reality. I'd learned to stop fighting other people; maybe it was finally time to stop fighting myself.

Standing in front of the mirror once again, I spoke my thoughts aloud.

"It's time to believe in yourself.

"It's okay to see yourself as you are and accept your body as it really is.

"It's okay to like yourself, to love yourself."

I sat on the floor, sobbing, feeling a freedom in my tears. As the tension left my chest and my shoulders relaxed, I felt my relationship to polio, and to myself, shift. The veil of denial fell away as I finally confronted what was currently happening to me and to my body. The doctors were telling me to take it easy and hope for the best, to rest my body to preserve what little might remain. The literature all pointed in the same direction. Rather than 'use it or lose it,' the researchers recommended slowing down, taking naps, and guarding what functions I did have.

I struggled once again, this time against the medical advice. I recognized that I might actually die from this disease I had escaped as a child, but for once, I faced it head on. My cavalier attitude toward risk had been a denial of my mortality. Yes, I might die from this, but in this moment I was still alive. While resting might be the correct course of action for some, it wasn't going to be the direction I chose.

Never one to give up, I couldn't see myself starting now. I couldn't imagine a life spent taking it easy; that would feel like I was just waiting for it to be over. My lethargy lifting, I found myself eager to get moving. No longer motivated by selfishness or recklessness, but by a healthy compassion for myself, I rejected the Post Polio worldview and made my decision to live what life I had left as fully as possible.

"If it's going to happen, it's going to happen anyway, so I may as well take the next two years and do what I damn well feel like. I don't need to roll over and give in; screw that. I've got a short time and a long bucket list."

1985

Rotary International launches PolioPlus, the first and largest internationally coordinated private-sector support of a public health initiative, with an initial pledge of $120 million.

CHAPTER 13

Top of my list was getting back to riding. No longer fearful of an accident, I figured I was living on borrowed time anyway. One of my first purchases was a used Gold Wing GL1100, and working with my father, we attached a Craig Vetter designed sidecar. Remembering my dad's modifications on my old Honda 50, I looked for a way to help me shift. The Wing's gas tank was separate from the fairing, which gave me the space I needed to run a rod down to the foot lever, put a link bearing in place, and connect a shifter I could use with my left hand while still being able to pull in the clutch handle at the same time. All that remained was getting my motorcycle endorsement added to my driver's license.

"You can't take the endorsement test with a sidecar attached," the man at the Department of Motor Vehicles said in his official sounding voice.

"Well, I can't really do that, now can I?" I replied. "I'm not going to ride a bike without one, so why shouldn't I take the test with one? Besides, I've ridden a bike since I was thirteen; I've just paused for a few years. It's not like I don't know what I'm doing."

He looked at me across the counter and paused for a moment. Taking in my crutches and the brace on my leg, he relented. "Well, if you get 100 percent on the written test, I'll give you the endorsement. Just don't go telling everyone what I did."

I passed the test easily and went out for my first ride in almost twenty years, leaving Robyn with her mother and taking a week off from work. Having ridden when I was younger, I assumed it would all come back to me instantly. I quickly discovered I was wrong; I'd forgotten some of the nuances of a bike that made it different than a car. Cruising across Nevada on US50, I misjudged the quality of the pavement and hit a bump, throwing me in the air and catching my right leg on the seat.

"Damn, here we go again!" My left leg dragged on the ground and my pants tore as I struggled to keep the bike under control. While I desperately tried to come to a stop, the sidecar kept everything from flipping over. Finally successful, I sat for a moment, catching my breath, dangling raggedly, half on, half off the bike. I looked down at my exposed leg and noticed my brace was scraped from the pavement. For once, I was grateful to be wearing it, not knowing what would have happened to my foot without it.

Righting myself, I got off the bike and checked to make sure everything was okay, including me. I tucked my shredded pant leg into my boot, climbed back on and sat for a moment, gathering my thoughts. *Perhaps reacquainting myself with riding might take a bit longer than I anticipated,* I thought, pondering my options.

Well, hell, if I'm going to end up in a wheelchair anyway, I may as well spend my last days of freedom having some fun. Rejecting any notion of slowing down to relearn how to ride, I gunned the engine and took off.

Once on the bike, I couldn't stop, riding 7,400 miles in the first seven days. I headed down Highway 50 in Nevada, ending up on Interstate 70 in Utah. I turned on every road I saw, dirt or paved, just to see where it would take me. I visited all the National Parks in Utah, camping for the night when fatigue finally hit, and felt no desire to go home.

Everywhere I went people approached me, curious about the bike and sidecar. I loved the spontaneity of our conversations, often learning as much about their adventures as they did about mine. My attention was drawn less and less to my body and fatigue, and once again I found myself composing music, singing aloud, or mulling over books I had read. My early years spent in long solitary hours with only my thoughts for company was now an asset. The miles flew by, putting in eight hundred to thousand mile days with little effort.

This is how I wanted it to be: to come skidding in at the end of my life. I could feel the grin stretching across my face as the life that had been draining from me returned. I no longer worried about Post Polio syndrome; I only worried about where to find the next gas station.

I began riding every weekend, going as far as I could before turning back toward home and work. Occasionally, Sonja or Robyn came with me, but most often I was alone while they spent time with their mother. Self-employed, I had control of my schedule. I decided to take a month off, get on the Wing and keep moving, continuing my exploration of each road that presented itself along the way.

I'd once read an article about a couple near New Orleans who owned and restored carousel horses. When I contacted them, they invited me to stay with them in the guest room housed above their garage should I ever come to the city. Planning one of my trips to route me through the south, I took them up on their offer.

"Here's a key, come and go as you'd like," they instructed. "We're sure you'll want to spend some time in the city. Just park your bike in the garage when you get back. Don't worry how late it is, we won't hear a thing."

I headed to the French Quarter, leaving the bike on a side street while I wandered around the historic area, checking out the local music scene. But walking back to my rig in the dark, I sensed a creeping panic starting to envelop my body.

What was going on? I hadn't been this afraid of the dark since I was a lot younger. Why now? My heart was racing and I was gasping for breath. The feeling intensified. I leaned against a wall, trying to regain my composure. Looking around me, I noticed every shadow, jumping when anything moved. *What the hell is this?*

Vampires. Fueled by the stories my mother had shared when I was little, images of vampires suddenly overwhelmed me. I saw them everywhere. Shocked by this awareness, I felt like a fool, glad no one was around to see my reaction. *You idiot! Vampires aren't real. Get a grip*, I admonished myself. *Get moving and get yourself to bed, this is ridiculous.* Despite my embarrassment, I had a hard time shaking the notion that I might be grabbed. I slowly made it to the bike and headed back to my room.

A few days later, I rented a car to tour more of the area. Discovering an old, vacant plantation, I parked in the dirt in front of the house and explored the dilapidated building. Cobwebs hung from the walls and ceilings, and the floorboards creaked as I ventured farther into the once stately home. Despite the light outside, some of the interior rooms were surprisingly dark. Walking down a long, narrow hallway toward what must have been a storage pantry I felt the now familiar flood of anxiety. Heart racing, palms sweating, and eyes blurring, I sat on the floor, trying to catch my breath. The vampires were back again.

You have to face this or you'll be forever fearful and captive to your imagination. Yes, this place is creepy and it reminds you of those old stories, but why are they coming back now after all these years? Maybe they've been there all along, just hidden too deeply to bother you before now. But whatever the reason, it's time to deal with them. You can't be worrying about creatures coming at you in the dark like you did as a kid. Seriously, this is ridiculous!

I knew I couldn't outrun the demons that might be lurking inside my mind. I had to confront my fears once and for all.

"Fine. Come out and show yourselves. I'm not afraid." The shaking in my voice betrayed my facade of confidence. "I know you aren't real. I know the stories are fantasies." The longer I spoke to the darkness, the more my breathing returned to normal. Soon, I was laughing at my situation. I had conquered the vampires; they had finally disappeared, never again to scare me.

After my first month off, I planned to take another, working in between to replenish my bank account and spend time with the girls. Having read once about the Chesapeake Bay and the characters that inhabited some of the more remote sections, I wanted to see it for myself. I decided to ride to the east coast, find a crabber, and convince him to take me out with him. I had no idea how I might do that, but was confident I'd figure it out once I got there.

Crossing into Maryland, I caught up with a couple riding a Harley Davidson, decked out from head to toe in leather gear and ¾ helmets. "Is there a campground anywhere near here?" I shouted to them as I slowed alongside. Indicating he couldn't understand what I was saying, he waved at me to follow, and led me to a nearby McDonald's.

He hopped off the bike and stuck out his hand. "Name's Dickie, and this is my wife, Lois." Inside, he ordered coffee for all of us, ignoring me as I pulled out my wallet, not letting me pay.

"I noticed your California license. Must have taken you ages to ride out here." They were stunned when I told them how many miles I had ridden in such a short a time, especially when I shared the many detours I had taken before arriving in Maryland. We chatted pleasantly for a few more minutes.

"What do you folks do for a living?" I inquired.

"We're crabbers," Dickie replied. I almost fell off my chair.

"Seriously? I came out here to see if I could go crabbing. I've read about it and have been dying to try it myself. Do you ever take people out with you? I'll pay for the chance," I added, hoping that would entice him.

Instead, he got mad. "How dare you suggest paying! That's an insult. Don't ever talk to me about money again. You come along with us, and you can camp in our yard. We'll show you what crabbing is like."

I couldn't believe my luck. Lois returned from the restroom just in time to hear Dickie's offer of a spot in their yard for my tent.

"Dickie! Where are your manners? Bob, I'd be offended if you refuse to stay in our spare bedroom, " she said, looking at the rain that had begun falling outside. "You just follow us on your bike and we'll make up the bed for you."

Three a.m. the next morning came quickly. "Time to go; got to get out and get going. Got a long day ahead of us." They hustled me to get ready and hurried me out to the boat in the dark.

Dickie wasn't joking. Pushing away from the dock by 4:30, we spent the day checking trotlines, pulling up pots and tossing chicken necks into empty ones to attract the crabs. My job was to net the crabs when we found them, hauling the net into the boat where we measured their size and determined their sex, tossing back any that were too small or female. Soft shell crabs were the most desirable, bringing in the greatest money. It was after 3 p.m. when we came back alongside the weathered pier, exhausted from a hard day's work. I stayed for four days, and returned many more times to visit over the years. Still crabbing into their seventies, they've remained good friends.

"Good day, ma'am," I called out to the woman sweeping her porch in the sultry heat of the Louisiana bayou. "I've been dying for some genuine Cajun food, home cooked, not restaurant style. I wonder if there'd be any chance you'd be willing to cook something for me. I'd be very happy to pay you restaurant price for it."

"Well, honey, you just park that motorcycle over there in the yard and come on in. My husband and son will be back any minute and I'll see what we can do for you." She pointed to a small patch of dirt just beyond her house.

Pulling out my crutches from the sidecar, I walked up the hard packed dirt to her porch, climbed the stairs and went inside. A small three-room house with a hole in one corner for spitting out tobacco, it was neat and cozy.

She fixed an amazing jambalaya, accompanied with fresh crawdads and catfish, and refused to take a dime. Joined by her husband and young son, we spent a pleasant evening talking about life on the bayou and compared it with life on the road until it was time for me to head out, thanking them profusely for their hospitality.

As I rode away, I reflected on people's willingness to welcome me, a complete stranger, into their homes and their private lives. I'd read somewhere that motorcycles with a sidecar were less intimidating; that instead of provoking fear of a rogue biker gang member, it invoked curiosity. Folks were more inclined to come up and ask questions about the rig, and my crutches immediately signaled I wasn't a threat. Even though I rode a motorcycle, I was clean cut, well-mannered, and respectful.

~

Robyn, my youngest, loved riding with me. Convincing Betty to let me take her on an extended bike vacation when she was thirteen, we spent well over a month exploring many of the back roads I had yet to see. With our gear stowed in the saddlebags and sidecar, she sat contentedly behind me on the bike, enjoying the scenery and the chance for an adventure. Stopping to camp late one night, we were awakened by the flap of our tent being torn open and a shrieking voice of woman yelling at us in the dim light of dawn.

"What the hell are you doing in my yard?" Without realizing it, we'd pitched our tent on her perfectly mowed front lawn. "You, I'd let starve, but I can't just let the kid go hungry. Seeing as your already here, you may as well come inside for some breakfast," she shrugged, walking back to her door.

In Cape Hatteras, I watched Robyn run across the beach and play in the surf. That evening, I noticed her feet were swollen, and looking more closely, I saw thousands of tiny red blotches. Sand fleas had bitten every inch of her ankles. Needing to press on, she rode sidesaddle the next day, her feet in a bucket of ice in the sidecar until we could get them once again to fit inside her boots.

Visiting a friend in Key West, I let Robyn lose on Duvall Street to wander the shops and explore on her own for a bit. Not long after, I saw her running toward me, turning to look behind her as if being chased.

"Dad, see that guy back there? He came out of that store and offered me money if I'd go away with him! He freaked me out!" she yelled, panting to catch her breath.

I dashed down the street. "I hope you weren't really thinking about propositioning my daughter, now were you?" I confronted the man, the anger on my face conveying the seriousness of my intent. Taking one look at my five-foot arms, he went back inside and didn't bother us again.

Robyn and I added a stop in Washington, DC, on our tour. DARE, or Drug Abuse Resistance Education, was holding a national kickoff event and when it became common knowledge how far we had travelled on the motorcycle, I was invited to be one of the guest speakers. Over the years, as a musician, I'd seen many talented people fall into trouble with drugs and alcohol. I saw how easily it could happen and kept my distance from most substances, only drinking occasionally, until well into my thirties. My own brief first marriage was an additional reminder of the dangers of the unintended consequences of overconsumption. Wanting to help kids, including my own, avoid the same destructive path as many of my friends, I'd started volunteering for DARE while on my break from Rotary.

Robyn didn't have much in the way of riding gear, so we avoided weather extremes as much as possible, stopping to camp if storms threatened. Late one afternoon, somewhere in New Mexico, we got caught unexpectedly in pelting, freezing rain. Even in a leather jacket with a down vest underneath, I was being torn to shreds. Passing one of the few hotels along the stretch of highway and seeing yet another 'No Vacancy" sign, I had no choice but to keep going. Finally I spotted a grungy, ragged hotel a small ways off the main road and pulled in, desperate for a room. In luck, I grabbed the keys from the clerk and led Robyn, lips blue and teeth chattering, straight to the shower to get her warm as fast as I could. Feeling like a terrible father, I tucked her into one of the tiny twin beds and laid down on the other.

"I think I could have gone another hundred miles, Dad," she said as she began to nod off. My heart swelled with pride. Motorcycling was the one of the only times I felt completely free, like I was getting away with something, something I wasn't supposed to be able to do. I assumed that I'd grow up and drive a car, but I never dreamed I'd ride a motorcycle, let alone with a passenger, and that the passenger would one day be my own daughter.

My annual month-long rides continued. Working long hours most of the year, I rode equally hard during my breaks. Weather, distance, and bad roads never deterred me. One fall, riding over 7 Mile Bridge between Knight's Key and Little Duck Key in Florida, a local law enforcement officer pulled me over.

"What are you doing riding in this rain? Don't you know a hurricane is bearing down on us?" He looked at me sternly.

"Well, sir, I know Hurricane Hugo is swiftly approaching, and my plan was to get to the mainland before it hits," I replied politely.

"You'll never make it. You're risking getting blown around, hit by flying debris, or worse. You need to get off the road, and you need to do it now!" he insisted.

"I appreciate your concern, Officer. But if you look, you'll see that truck over there, shattered by lightning. Aren't the odds just as bad that I will be hit in motion the same as if I were still? I think I'll just keep going, if you don't mind." My tone clearly indicated I had no intention of stopping. Not knowing how to respond, and having no legal reason to hold me, he simply got back in his car, shaking his head. I kept going, escaping the worst of the storm as I rode north.

Exhausted from the never-ending rain, the next evening just outside Tallahassee, Florida, I circumnavigated a giant flood of water to park my bike on the only portion of the shabby hotel lot that was dry. Dripping water from every surface as I went into the office to get a room, the desk clerk, an aging hippie biker, quoted the price, $14 per night.

"But I'm not so sure you want to stay here," he said, despite my obvious desire for rest.

"Hey, buddy, I'm bone tired, I just need a bed and a roof over my head. It can't be that bad."

"Your choice." He handed me the keys.

Unable to find the light switch, I walked slowly across the damp floor, feeling for the bathroom where I hoped I'd find a switch.

What a crappy place, I thought. *The guy was right, it even floods inside.*

I flipped on the light and slowly realized every single surface of the room was covered in green; as my eyes adjusted, the surfaces were moving. I had not been stepping on squishy, moist carpet but on frogs, hundreds of them, everywhere I looked.

"Holy shit!" I yelled, not caring how many I killed as I ran from the room.

"Tried to warn ya," was all he said, a sly grin on his face as he handed me back my $14.

~

Shiprock, in the remote northwest corner of New Mexico, has few hospitality services. Needing to stop for the night, I noticed two diners across the street from one another. I chose the one with the full parking lot, usually a sign of better food, to grab a bite to eat and see if anyone knew of a good place to camp. Approached by a woman with greasy hair, perhaps three remaining teeth, and a body that would smother me if given the chance, she suggested I stay in the city park.

"Make sure you park your bike under the bridge, honey," she purred as she gave directions to the city center.

"Why? The weather looks clear tonight; the bike should be okay," I answered.

"Well, honey, I thought after work I'd come see you," she smiled suggestively.

Smiling back, I finished my meal, paid my bill, and hopped on the bike. I didn't stop moving until I was in the next state.

~

My fear of the wheelchair faded into the background. My body had stabilized and the doctors' worst predictions were not coming to pass. The greater risks to my life continued to be self-inflicted. Riding the Wing around town I rarely, if ever, wore a helmet, believing it was only necessary for longer trips. One afternoon as I headed for the practice room to audition a new drummer for one of the two bands I was managing, a voice inside my head kept nagging me: put on a helmet. Usually one to ignore such thoughts, I turned around and grabbed my three-quarter helmet from the garage, which covered my head but not my face. Taking off again, I made it halfway down the block before returning once more to put on the full-face helmet I used only for cross-country rides.

The squeal of the brakes registered in my mind just before I felt the impact of the truck as it t-boned into the sidecar. The driver had failed to stop for the red light and plowed into me at full speed, the force of the blow shoving the handlebar of the Wing into the temple of my helmet and shattering the protective chin bar. Awkwardly wedged on the bike, waiting for the emergency crew to disentangle me and take me to the hospital to confirm the bike and helmet were the only things damaged, I vowed to never again ride anywhere without a full-face helmet.

Camping with Sonja and Robyn (1986)

Crabbing in Chesapeake Bay

1988

The World Health Assembly passes a resolution
to eradicate polio by the year 2000,
and the Global Polio Eradication Initiative is launched.

CHAPTER 14

Given my previous unsuccessful marriages, I was eager to date but not interested in any form of commitment, and with ample opportunity to meet women at my music gigs, I took full advantage of my freedom. Still scrupulously honest about my intentions, I entertained numerous brief relationships but took none very seriously. Dating, motorcycling, and parenting the girls consumed most of my spare time, and I was enjoying my life.

In addition to motorcycles, I'd always had a fascination with older cars, and got involved in the Imperial Owners of Sacramento Valley Car Club. At a car show at the Nut Tree Hotel in Vacaville in my role as president of the club, I found myself in a conversation about music with a man named Terry. His wife, Patti, stood next to him smoking a cigarette and flicking her poodle cut hair with her free hand. Mentioning Terry's excellent mechanical skills, she wondered if I'd be willing to swap his car services for restoring their piano, and our friendship grew over the next several months.

Bringing my car for servicing one afternoon, I arrived at their house and knocked on the door.

"Who is it?" I heard Terry's voice from somewhere in the house.

"It's me, Bob. Brought the car as we arranged the other day," I yelled through the closed door. I waited several minutes before it opened a crack. For some reason Terry was reluctant to open it any farther, and when he poked his head out, I noticed his hair was disheveled and he had a surprised expression on his face. Behind him, I saw a woman I'd never met scrambling to tie the knot on a robe as she skirted across the living room and into the bathroom.

"Um, I must have confused the days. I was expecting you tomorrow. I'm working at home today, and the place is a mess or I'd invite you in. Just give me the keys and I'll take care of everything." The calmness in his voice attempted to mask his shaking hand as he thrust it through the sliver of the open door.

I was stunned by his blatant lie. Without thinking, I dropped the keys, not caring where they landed. I heard them clattering on the ground as I turned and walked back toward the street, wanting only to get away as quickly as possible. I didn't even think about how I would get back home; I just wanted to leave, shocked at what I had just witnessed.

It took until the next morning for me to calm down enough to call him about my car. When I finally had the nerve to speak with him, I was furious at his betrayal of Patti. "What the hell were you doing?" I yelled. "What was that woman doing in your house? What's the hell's going on?"

"As soon as I can get a divorce from Patti, I'm going to marry that woman," he informed me. "I've been unhappy for a long time. Besides, it's none of your business anyway. This is between Patti and me."

"Does Patti know about any of this? Have you even talked to her?" I was stunned by his cavalier attitude. All I could think about was Patti. She'd been only kind and caring when I'd visited, and I hadn't seen any signs of trouble between them. She was a good person and didn't deserve this treatment. If he was going to be an ass, I could at least be there for her.

"She's going to need someone to help her if you go through with this. I'd like to be that friend," I managed to spit out. Surprisingly, he didn't argue.

I called Patti and she reluctantly agreed to meet with me at a local coffee shop. Bringing up what I had witnessed, and knowing Terry had finally told her he wanted a divorce, I blurted out, "Patti, do you want to stay married to Terry? Are you happy?"

"No, not really. I'm not happy," she confessed. "I guess a divorce is the right thing, I just didn't expect it to end like this," she slowly opened up, relieved to have someone to talk to.

Over the next few months we talked more, sharing stories of our marriages, as well as our hopes and dreams for the future when we met for occasional lunches and dinners. It was clear we both appreciated our growing friendship and I found myself looking forward to our times together.

"Thanks for stealing my wife, Bob." Terry's phone call and bitter accusations slammed me out of the blue. "You're the reason we're divorcing, you know."

I was stunned. Where was this coming from? He was the one who wanted out, and now here he was completely distorting the facts. It was obvious he had no interest in discussing the issue, and even less interest in what had actually occurred, but at least Patti and I knew the truth. His version of the story only cemented our growing bond.

Soon Patti and I were spending most of our time together, realizing we had a lot in common and enjoyed each other's company. I noticed that I felt comfortable, and found myself becoming more open and emotionally honest with her in a way I had never done before. I felt safe being myself, and before long it was hard to imagine a future in which she wasn't present. As we grew closer, we slowly integrated our children into our relationship, making sure they would be included in any plans we might make in the future.

"Patti, will you marry me?" I had finally found my perfect partner. For the first time, I knew exactly what I was doing.

"Yes, Bob, I'd be honored." We were married on April 22, 1992.

~

Robyn, who had lived with me since the divorce, stayed with us for the first years of our marriage. She moved out to spend time with her mother during her last semester of high school but came by often to spend time with us. Patti's daughter, Heather, twelve at the time we blended families, opted to stay with her father, while Josh, ten, moved in with us. Weekends when all the kids were around were chaotic but fun as they all got along well.

A few years earlier, when Sonja had turned nineteen, Betty requested she be granted sole responsibility for her care. I agreed, reasoning Betty had been her primary parent while I had mainly spent weekends and vacations with her. Unfortunately, over the years following that decision, Betty slowly encouraged Sonja to limit her visits with me, and soon the frequency of our time together decreased substantially. To this day, a major regret I have is that I didn't understand the implications of what seemed to be a simple procedural motion and that I didn't figure out a way to fight harder to have an ongoing relationship with my oldest daughter, believing at that time it was in Sonja's best interests for me to avoid any conflict with her mother.

Patti and me (1994)

1994

The World Health Organization Region of the Americas is certified polio-free. In China, 80 million children are vaccinated.

1997

The last case of wild polio occurs in
the World Health Organization Western Pacific Region—
a fifteen-month-old girl in Cambodia.

CHAPTER 15

"Bob, when are you going to go back to Rotary?" Patti's question caught me off guard. "You talk about it all the time, yet you haven't gone to a meeting as long as I've known you. It doesn't make sense to me."

Amidst the turmoil of my Post Polio diagnosis, I'd stopped all involvement, and had yet to return. Encouraging me to revisit my relationship with Rotary, Patti suggested I attend a luncheon meeting.

"It was incredible, Patti. It was like I never left," I shared after my first meeting. "I had no idea how much I missed going. I was welcomed back with open arms, and the other members were already talking about what committees I can get on. There's something about this organization that fills my soul."

My time volunteering elsewhere had been productive, but not as deeply rewarding as the work I had done with Rotary. It felt good to be back, and before long I had worked my way through local and district committees, finally landing on several statewide initiatives. Patti fully supported my involvement, attending meetings with me and establishing friendships with everyone she met. Rather than Rotary functioning as an escape from my marriage, it was becoming interwoven into the fabric of the life we were creating together.

On a short break from emceeing the program and providing entertainment for the West Sacramento Rotary Club's Anniversary dinner, I sat down at a table with Luann Crist, the wife of the club's president, Bob Collins. As we chatted about our various activities, she brought up my motorcycling.

"Bob, what ride are you going to do this year?" she inquired, familiar with my annual motorcycling sabbaticals.

"Well, I'm thinking about riding to all forty-eight state capitals in a thirty-day window. I'm not sure if anyone's done it before, and it sounds like a fun trip." I took a sip from my glass of wine.

"Are you doing it for charity?"

"No, just a personal goal I've had. Thought it would be a good challenge for me, something to keep me busy this summer," I answered honestly. "I just like to get away on an adventure, take a break from work."

"Have you thought about riding it for PolioPlus?" Luann suggested.

PolioPlus was the top fundraising focus of our club but I hadn't paid much attention to the details, nor really, had I paid much attention to polio. I could recite the facts and figures, but in the same way I could recite other facts and figures about the activities of Rotary.

The last documented case of endemic polio occurred in the US in 1979, the same year The Rotary Foundation funded a grant to provide immunizations for over six million children in the Philippines, thus starting Rotary's commitment to the world wide eradication of polio.

Rotary's program, PolioPlus, and their fundraising efforts on its behalf, caught the attention of the World Health Assembly, which went on to resolve, through the Global Polio Eradication Initiative, to end polio by the year 2000.

Prior to 1988, when the Global Polio Eradication Initiative was started, more than 350,000 people a year were paralyzed by the disease. The efforts on behalf of polio eradication have resulted in an almost 99 percent decrease in cases worldwide.

"What a great idea!" I slapped my hand on the table—almost knocking over my wine—surprising Luann with my sudden burst of enthusiasm. "I never would have thought of that. I've never done anything for charity on a scale like that, but I'm sure it can be done. Let's figure out a way to make it happen. Are you interested in helping?"

I hadn't put it together before that my riding might benefit PolioPlus, the number one fundraising focus of Rotary. The minute she mentioned it I could see the entire picture taking shape in my mind. I believed deeply in our motto, 'Service Above Self,' and I wanted to help a good cause. Combining my passions—riding and Rotary—was a natural, and if my forty-eight state capital ride might bring greater attention to our work, I was delighted to help.

Forming a committee with over thirty volunteers to help with logistics, including contacting Rotary groups in each capital to let them know I was coming, the plans quickly came together. The goal was to raise awareness of our campaign at each stop, not to solicit direct donations. We arranged for some light media coverage in a few of the capitals, thinking they might help us broaden the knowledge of Rotary's work beyond the membership of local clubs. Patti and I thought a nickname might help identify me as I rode from state to state, and we chose 'Motorcycle Bob'; simple, obvious, and easy to remember.

"If I wait until June to leave I should hit good weather most of the trip. Heat I can handle; snow would be a problem." I showed

Patti my planned route, zigzagging through the various states, taking into account the timing necessary to ensure witnesses would be able to meet me at each stop. "If I can keep to this schedule I'll be in good shape."

Final preparations were completed, the bike was packed, and the local media was invited to witness my departure. Just prior to leaving, the group gathered for well wishes and a few speeches assembled in front of the state capital in Sacramento.

"As Motorcycle Bob begins his journey to raise awareness of our mission, I'd like to take a moment to award him with the Ruby Paul Harris Award, given to members who have made a significant impact on the work of Rotary. Congratulations, Bob, and good luck on your ride." Cliff Dochterman, a past Rotary International World President, handed me the plaque.

Surprised and deeply moved, I thanked everyone who had come to see me off. I climbed onto the bike, settled on the seat, and started the engine. Smiling for the photographers and kissing Patti goodbye, I gave her the award for safekeeping. Then I drove my Gold Wing through the ceremonial start ribbon they held across the street and began my odyssey, smiling quietly to myself. Fifty years since I had contracted polio, I reflected on the wild twists and turns my life had taken; from being told I might never walk again to riding a motorcycle solo across the US, my heart was full of joy and gratitude.

If one wants to have a good laugh, make plans that assume good weather. I was barely out of Sacramento before hitting signs warning of flashfloods ahead. Taking my chances, I made it through without incident, only to be slammed by blowing snow, 28-degree temperatures, and relentless headwinds from Pocatello, Idaho, all the way to Helena, Montana. I'd only been on the road three days.

Freezing, I pulled up to the capital building in Helena, alone. I'd expected to be met by at least a few Rotarians, and now, had to figure out how to document my arrival. Seeing a woman bundled tightly against the cold, I asked her to take a photo. "And would you mind signing my booklet as a witness?"

"Sure, but let's hurry. My fingers are nearly frostbitten!" Working as fast as we could in the bitter cold, she snapped the picture and waited patiently while I pulled out the homemade passport book Patti and I had made before my departure. She wrote her name and address on the designated lines, then shook her head. "You know you're crazy, right?" Bundling up, she scurried off to find warmth in a nearby coffee shop. I stuffed the book and camera back into the safety of my side case, climbed back on the bike, and headed south. The headwinds turned into tailwinds and the snow changed to thunderstorms with lightning flashing in the distance. *This has to get better!* I kept telling myself. I had to catch a break sometime soon.

Apparently it wasn't going to be in Salt Lake City. Relieved to be greeted by fellow Rotarian Dave Pollei, who took my photo despite the relentless downpour, I welcomed a good night's sleep in a warm bed. The following morning, I attended a press conference as well as an interview and photo shoot with a local syndicated Internet-TV host, James Brown, which delayed my departure. I was already behind schedule.

After another day of snow, hail, rain, and 680 miles of riding, I arrived late in Denver and found a Belgian tourist willing to take my photo before I headed north again to Cheyenne. Cold gave way to heat in Wisconsin. Averaging 700 miles or more a day, the warmth was welcome at first. But extremes of weather seemed to follow me. Soon I was sweltering in 106-degree temperatures, while once again battling wind and rain. Stuck in the poor conditions for well over 100 miles, and drenched to the bone, I found a hotel in Fort Smith, Arkansas, where I was able to dry off both my cell phone and myself.

As I entered the city limits of Frankfort, Kentucky, I was startled to see two sheriff's officers awaiting me and wondered what I had done to warrant their lights and sirens. I was relieved when they pulled in front of me to escort me to the capital. The Rotary club was out in force, and the mayor proclaimed June 11th "Bob Mutchler Day." The following morning I participated in a thirty-minute cable interview along with Bill Miller, formerly of the World Health Organization. Word about PolioPlus was spreading.

I stayed an extra day to clean and do maintenance on the bike and watched as the evening brought eighty mile-per-hour winds, three-inch hailstones, more rain, and tornados to the area. Grateful for the layover day and the chance to miss the storm, I made my plans to leave early the next morning for Lansing, Michigan, and then on to Indianapolis, Indiana, where Rotary International was convening for their annual conference. As I drove up to the convention center, Cliff Dochterman greeted me and showed me where they had arranged to park my motorcycle, putting it on display for the attendees to see in between sessions. The next afternoon he welcomed me to the stage at the Paul Harris Fellowship Luncheon.

"I'd like to introduce our fellow Rotarian, Bob Mutchler. He's been riding to the state capitals to raise awareness of the mission of PolioPlus to those outside of Rotary. He's going to take a few minutes to share his story, and he's even agreed to play a song for us to conclude this session today. I'm sure you'll all enjoy his chat. Come on up, Bob!"

I spent the rest of the day talking to small groups of members as they walked around my bike, selling PolioPlus bumper stickers, and making connections that might be helpful for the remainder of the trip. It was a pleasant, brief break from riding.

Strangers often approached me when I stopped for food and gas, curious about the sidecar and the stickers plastered all over it. Fellow motorcycle riders struck up conversations about my route, the distances I was travelling, and what it was like to cover so many miles in such a short time. Every once in a while I noticed a different type of rider, a kindred spirit who understood my experiences without needing an explanation. Swapping knowing glances, our stories were about the joys of riding for hours, alone with only oneself for company; about covering endless miles without the need for stopping; riders for whom a thousand-mile day meant nothing. As word spread of my journey, more of these riders came to the press conferences, and through them I got my first introduction to a previously unknown organization, the Iron Butt Association, a group dedicated to safe, long-distance motorcycling.

"There he is! Hey, Bob!" I couldn't hear their shouts, but I recognized the friendly waves as I crossed into New York State. Three Rotarians on their own bikes had been waiting alongside the road to greet me, and as I rode past they pulled in behind me. Together we rode over one hundred miles in the pouring rain to Albany, where a huge crowd began cheering as we pulled up. Three proclamations, a 3-D photo of the capital, a few t-shirts, and a $1000 donation for PolioPlus later, I headed on to Pennsylvania.

Riding into Charlotte, North Carolina, I took a shortcut and found myself on a pitch-black road, barely able to see in front of me. Suddenly, something slammed into my foot, searing pain shot through my body and tears sprung to my eyes. I didn't feel safe stopping in the dark, so I rode on an additional sixty miles until I found a streetlight. Stopping to inspect the damage, I pulled owl feathers and guts from my gear and footpeg. My foot, severely swollen, wouldn't come out of the boot for several days.

Patti rode her bike over from Folsom and joined me for the final stop in Carson City, Nevada. We gathered our gear and walked together into the Hardman Hotel. I wanted to get a good night's sleep before getting back on the bike and heading to the capital building where the local media, along with numerous Rotary members, celebrated the completion of my journey.

As we rode through the Sierras on our return to Folsom, I was already planning my next trip. I was tired, but I was also excited. In almost every city Rotarians opened their homes, their businesses, and their hearts, helping me gain publicity, food, accommodations, needed repairs for the bike, and encouragement. Planning my route with precision, arranging witnesses to meet me at each capital to take my photo and sign my book, demanded I keep to a strict schedule. But failing to account for time zone changes, I often arrived late for the press conferences we had pre-arranged. A coolant leak, balding tires, traffic snarls, and unplanned interviews in previous towns often meant having to find a cooperative stranger to help me out when the scheduled witnesses gave up and headed home. With the lone exception of Pierre, South Dakota, where I used the time delay feature on my camera to snap my own photo, I had my witness book signed in every capital. Each interview I gave produced more questions, and each station wanted its own coverage of the event. Callers asked where they could send money, and PolioPlus was the recipient of all the good will. Along the way I realized the impact my riding could have and the unique contribution I could make to Rotary.

Cliff Dochterman cutting the ribbon on my first ride for PolioPlus (1998)

My old Gold Wing with custom gearshift (1998)

1998

In Turkey, a thirty-three-month-old unvaccinated child
is the last child paralyzed by wild poliovirus
in the European Region.

1999

The United Nations Secretary-General agrees to negotiate truces
for immunization in the Democratic Republic of Congo.
National Immunization Days are conducted in war-torn Liberia.

CHAPTER 16

Standing outside the headquarters of the California Highway Patrol, or CHP, with a group of Rotarians, fellow officers, and friends, I watched the BMW executives gather around the brand new 1999 R1100RT. Parked between two patrol motorcycles, its bright blue paint stood out from their standard black and white. Having conquered the lower forty-eight, I decided the next logical ride would be across Canada, our neighbor to the north. Dubbing it the TransCanada Motorcycle Ride, my agenda was once again to bring awareness to PolioPlus by meeting with Rotary groups as I made my east across the country.

"Okay, let's get this show on the road," commanded Dwight "Spike" Helmick, the CHP Commissioner and honorary chairperson of the 1999 PolioPlus Ride. He spoke to the assembled crowd about the impact of the Rotary program and the opportunities to support the efforts to eradicate polio going forward, finished his remarks, and invited me to the podium. I shared some of the highlights of my forty-eight state capitals in thirty days, or 48-30 ride, and the impressions I had of the reception to my appearances around the country.

"I'd now like to introduce Tony Felice from A&S BMW Motorcycles," Spike's voice boomed over the crowd as he returned to the podium. "Bob, stay up here as well."

Tony stepped to the microphone. "Bob, in honor of your ride, and your dedication to the work of Rotary and PolioPlus, I'm handing you the keys to this BMW RT. It's yours to use for this ride; the pink slip belongs to your Rotary club." Tony dropped the keys into my hand. "Dave and Ruth Hannigan have graciously donated the sidecar. It's a bit different than the one you've been using. Let them know what you think after you've ridden with it for a few miles."

Back again at the state capital building in Sacramento, as TV crews filmed the action, three CHP motorcycles and one patrol car—with lights flashing—escorted my friend Dave Boles and me to the county line, where we waved goodbye and headed north. This time, I had more to offer as I rode: in addition to the 'Goodbye Polio' bumper stickers and PolioPlus Ride pins, the sidecar was filled with a huge stock of Jelly Belly jelly beans, courtesy of Herman Goelitz's Jelly Belly store.

"Man, what a motorcycle! The RT is smooth and handles beautifully, and the leaner on this Hannigan is absolutely fantastic. It's the first time I've ever been able to ride like a solo bike!" Phoning Patti my first night out, I couldn't say enough about the new sidecar. "The name is appropriate: it lets the bike lean from side to side. I don't have to push it through the corners. I can only imagine this is a bit of what it feels like on two wheels." I was in love.

Dave rode along with me through Oregon, Washington, and crossing on the ferry to Victoria, Canada, and headed home when we hit Vancouver. As he turned south, I continued east, and once again I was on my own. Friendly people, helpful Rotarians, and rain greeted me at every stop.

"The Canadian government will match every dollar raised for polio immunization resulting from your ride," Patti informed me when I reached Prince George. "I hope Rotary International has enough PolioPlus pins to give to them!" We were both ecstatic. I didn't know about the pins lasting, but what I did have were Jelly Belly jelly beans, and many of the local clubs decided their sales would make excellent fundraisers for PolioPlus. The word was spreading and the Canadians were embracing my ride and the cause.

~

What was that? I shouted inside my head as the sidecar made a huge lurch. *What did I hit?* Must have been one of those potholes. I hadn't seen anything, but the asphalt was in poor shape in many places. Slowing, I moved toward the side of the road to assess the damage. It looked like the rear mounting bracket broke loose. I figured I could make it to Regina with it like that. Once I got into town someone might be able to help me get this fixed.

Driving into the city, I followed the directions to the local Rotary gathering. As I pulled up, a full-blown reception met me. I hadn't seen sun in eight days, my bike was a mess, and cameras were pointed at me: excellent first impression.

I had no choice but to pull my helmet off and shout out a greeting. "What a great reception. So happy to see all of you here today on behalf of PolioPlus."

Smiling, I gave interviews and answered questions, while behind the scenes, the club members worked diligently to locate a welder to fix the mounting bracket. They found one willing to work after his regular hours, who had it running in no time. The hospitality continued: a suite at a local hotel, a fine dinner with the club president's family, and a warm send-off the following morning rejuvenated me despite the never-ending rain.

The sun, finally making an appearance somewhere near Winnipeg, brought my awareness to the toll the damaged sidecar had taken on my rear tire. Almost threadbare, I limped into town and found a BMW dealer, Wild Wood Sports.

"It's your lucky day. We have one tire left that will fit your bike." I breathed a sigh of relief. "We'll get it changed in no time. Want the bike washed while we're at it?"

Gladly accepting their offer, I chatted with the salesmen while the shop finished their work. "Thanks for your help," I said, shaking everyone's hand. "I've got a press conference and interview with the Canadian Broadcast Company, and a later meeting with all nine Winnipeg Rotary Clubs, and the bike looks fantastic."

Visiting with clubs in the cities where I stopped, I was frequently presented with a check for PolioPlus, which I forwarded to The Rotary Foundation. The matching dollars from the Canadian government were quickly adding up, and I was continually surprised at the outpouring of support and enthusiasm wherever I went.

I now had a full beard, opting to skip shaving during the ride. I caught a glimpse of a TV interview I had given the night before and was shocked to see how scraggly I looked. Man, if that guy came up and asked me for money, I'd run like hell the other way! I took my Swiss Army knife into the hotel bathroom and hacked off as much hair as I could. I bought a razor at my next stop.

The rain and wind were my constant companions, with the exception of pea soup fog near Halifax, Nova Scotia. Thankfully, it cleared crossing Confederation Bridge, which at eight miles in length is the longest freestanding bridge in ice-infested waters in the world. A posse of Rotarian motorcyclists on Prince Edward Island greeted me as I came onto land and escorted me through the harbor and onto the town of Montague, where I spent the day speaking to the local club and swapping stories with other riders.

Crossing back to the mainland, I noticed a group of over sixty riders waiting for someone. Assuming they were looking for me, I pulled up to a policeman.

"Are you part of the group expecting me?" I inquired.

"No, we're looking for Motorcycle Bob," he replied, obviously unaware he was speaking to him. "I'm looking for the van he's coming in."

"Van?" I was surprised. "No, I'm here, I'm Motorcycle Bob, and this is my bike," I corrected him. "Where did get the idea I'd be in a van?"

He pulled out a copy of the local paper, unfolding it to an article about my ride. "Here, it says you're inside a van, riding a stationary bike, and that you have no arms and no legs." He handed me the paper. I was astounded. I'd spent four days talking with the reporter about my ride, my bike, and PolioPlus, and somehow he had misinterpreted everything I had said.

"Well, apparently you can't trust everything you read in the papers," I laughed, "because as you can see, I have all my limbs, I'm on a motorcycle, and there's no van."

He waved to signal my arrival, and the group revved their engines in unison. Following me in procession, we drove around before heading to a motorcycle dealership where the local Harley Owners Group donated a new tire for the bike in honor of PolioPlus.

When I crossed through US border customs in Maine, the agent started with the usual questions.

"Where have you been?"

"Riding across Canada for PolioPlus," I answered honestly, sure he would have no idea what that meant.

"Are you a Rotarian?" he inquired.

"Yes," I replied, surprised by his question. How could he have known? Was word spreading that far?

"Where are you going?" He seemed genuinely interested in my travels.

"Back home... California."

"Oh, my Dad's a Rotarian, in Yuba...." he paused.

"Yuba City?" I looked at him, surprised. What a small world. Yuba was less than fifty miles northwest of Folsom. What were the odds of meeting someone related at the far other end of the country?

"Yes," he replied, puzzled.

"What's his name?" Although the last name on his badge didn't look familiar, I wondered if I'd ever met him.

"Bill. I'm his youngest son, Roscoe. Well, buddy, if you're a Rotarian, you must be okay. Safe riding!" Waving, he passed me through.

I originally planned to finish my ride with a New York to San Francisco coast-to-coast world record time attempt, but instead swung through Illinois for an invited appearance that, unfortunately, didn't happen when signals got crossed. Disappointed, I hopped back on the bike and finished by riding non-stop back to Folsom, happy with the results of my Trans-Canada ride and my campaign to raise awareness for PolioPlus.

CHAPTER 17

Dear Mr. Kneebone,

I'm a motorcyclist with many thousands of miles under my belt. On behalf of Rotary and PolioPlus, I've ridden to all forty-eight state capitals in thirty days, and recently completed a Trans-Canada ride. I've met riders along the way who have told me stories of the Iron Butt Association. I have ridden numerous thousand-mile days, been to the four corners of the US, and went from coast-to-coast-to-coast although I never formally documented any of my rides. I recently heard about the eleven day, eleven thousand mile Iron Butt Rally. I believe my experiences qualify me and I would like to gain admission to your event as part of my awareness campaign for PolioPlus.

Thanks for your consideration,

Bob Mutchler

The Rally's tagline—eleven days, eleven thousand miles—seemed simple enough to me. Sharing my riding history with Mike Kneebone in a series of email exchanges, it was clear I could go the distance. The chance to increase awareness of the fight against polio was a compelling argument, and he granted my request.

I passed another rider on my way to Ojai, California, and the start of the Rally, and saw my first fuel cell, a welded metal container with hoses attached, secured to the passenger seat. Having no idea the level of sophistication of the competition, I was stunned to see auxiliary lights, heated gear, GPSs, computers, and various other accoutrements as I pulled into the parking lot of the hotel. Who were these people? Why did they need all this equipment?

A&S BMW had donated the blue R1100RT and Hannigan sidecar to my local Rotary club in 1999, and I had purchased it from them the following year. I had fifty-one paper maps, one for each state in the continental US and three for Canada, in my bag; a stock fuel tank; and a few layers of warm clothes.

"You don't have any heated gear? What the hell are you thinking?" During the pre-rally events, Dale Wilson, a veteran rider and current technical inspector for the Rally, approached me to talk about cold weather.

"I don't want your sorry ass suffering from hypothermia on my conscience," he continued. I ascertained very quickly Dale wasn't one to mince words. "I'm not sending you out without at least a heated vest. Use mine. You can hook it into your bike and when you get cold, turn it on and the wires inside will heat it up. It'll at least keep you from freezing to death." He walked away, muttering under his breath, only to reappear a few minutes later, vest in hand.

"Here's the wiring. Just hook it directly into the bike's battery. Should work fine." He set everything on the bike. "Let me know if you have any problems."

"Thanks, Dale. I should be okay." I set the vest in the sidecar, removed the RT's seat, and began working. It didn't take long to figure out the wiring, and I was soon heading into the hotel for dinner.

In the ballroom for the pre-Rally banquet, I chatted with a few of the other riders. Many were veterans, having completed numerous other rallies, and most paid little attention to me, an unknown rookie. Taking our seats, silence descended on the crowd as Mike Kneebone approached the podium.

"Okay, riders, we'll be handing out your rally packs and rally flags momentarily. As you know, the Iron Butt Rally is a giant scavenger hunt. To become a finisher in the 1999 Rally, you must ride to each of the four checkpoints, located in Washington State, Maine, Florida, and finally back here to California, a total distance of approximately 8,000 miles. You must arrive at each checkpoint in the time frame indicated in your packet. You are allowed to miss one, but if you miss a second, or come in after the time window closes, you will be disqualified." 8,000 miles seemed easy; I was planning on riding 13,000.

"Along the way, you'll be stopping to document bonuses, such as plaques or monuments, to prove you were in a certain place at a certain time," Mike continued. "This pack contains far more places to go then you could possibly get to in the time you have allowed. The first checkpoint will be in two days in Kennewick, Washington. You will be planning a route that will take you to as many bonus locations as you think you can get to, where you will take a picture of the described item with your flag in each photo. You are required to log the date, time, and odometer reading at each bonus stop, and you must keep a fuel log, also with date, time, number of gallons and odometer reading for every single gas stop you make. You will earn points for each bonus, but only if you don't mess it up."

Holy shit! What was he talking about? Bonuses? Fuel logs? I thought I only had to ride miles, not keep records, plan routes, or take photos. I'd read all the emails before the Rally, but hadn't really comprehended the concept of the ride. My intent was to ride a lot of miles over the eleven days. It hadn't occurred to me there was more to it.

I returned my attention back to Mike as he continued to rattle off information.

"The number one question about the rally is, 'What is the route

179

from checkpoint to checkpoint?' The answer is simple: there is no designated route. Each rider chooses the best way to get from checkpoint to checkpoint; that's what makes the Iron Butt a thinking person's game.

"The theme of this year's Rally is Tragedy, so you will be visiting sites memorializing toxic waste spills, floods, volcanic eruptions, meteor strikes, and nuclear meltdowns, as well as our usual mix of adding whatever we think makes the ride more interesting or challenging."

Lovely, I thought. *Disasters. I hope that isn't foreshadowing.*

Mike's voice filled the room. "For the first leg, you will need to 'Pick Your Poison.' You will have a choice of four routes, labeled Poisons 1-4. In this case, Poison #1 is the most direct route north from Ojai toward the Washington checkpoint. Poison #2 sends you south to downtown Los Angeles and then swings eastward toward Salt Lake City. #3 will take you through Nevada before taking you to Salt Lake City and then northwest back to Kennewick. Poison #4 sends you southeast to Tucson, Arizona. While you may visit bonuses in any order you want, you may not mix bonuses from one set of bonus listings. For example, if you choose the most direct route to Washington on Poison #1, you can NOT get credit for any bonuses on Poison #2, 3 or 4. To better explain this, here is a quote from Robert Higdon's 1997 Iron Butt Rally report where riders had to choose between a Canadian or United States route:

> *This style of rally construction is similar to eating in a Chinese restaurant. If you like the egg rolls in Column A, you can't have any wontons in Column B. A rider opting for the ride through Canada can pick up bonus points only from that route. And if, along the way, he comes within ten feet of a staggering bonus belonging to the U.S. route section, he has to pass it up. The contestant is forced to make difficult choices about route planning before leaving the checkpoint, knowing that a minute spent looking at a*

map right now could save two hours tomorrow. It isn't easy. It isn't supposed to be.

My mind was racing. How was I going to get off the bike, assuming I could even find the bonus, secure my flag to whatever it is I was required to show, take the Polaroid photo, document everything, then get back on the bike and make it to the next bonus? On the bike, I was equal to any rider. Off the bike, I was at a distinct disadvantage.

Catching me as I left the meeting, Mike advised, "Just run the base route, don't go for any bonuses. Just finish the Rally. Your goal is to raise awareness for PolioPlus; finishing will accomplish that." I nodded and went out into the hallway.

But I'm not willing to take the easy way out. I want to go for bonuses and I don't want any special treatment. I'll figure it out as I go. The conversation in my head was focused on one thing: *don't settle for simply riding the base route.* My mind made up, I went to my room to figure out which of the poison pills I was willing to swallow.

Poison #1's route headed north from Ojai, snaking over to the Pacific Coast Highway; a long, twisty, tourist-filled road this time of year. There were five bonuses to be gathered before leaving California, but, heeding Mike's advice, I opted to limit what I tackled in the first leg. Looking at my maps, I calculated the time it would take for the straight ride up Interstate 5 to Weed, California, where I would split off onto Highway 97 north before rejoining another interstate into Kennewick, a distance of 1,051 miles. If, instead, I went for a single, 400-point photo bonus in Washington State, I would add only 220 miles to my route but come into the checkpoint having scored at least one bonus. As I left the parking lot with the other riders early the next morning, I felt confident in my plan. What I had yet to learn was that the higher the points, the harder the riding.

What looked simple on paper proved to be far more challenging in real time. Driving up the road to Windy Ridge, overlooking Mount St. Helens, site of the volcanic eruption of May 18, 1980, freezing temperatures and snow patches greeted me as I climbed to the higher elevations. Grateful for Dale and his loan of the Widder vest, I turned it on, waiting for the eagerly anticipated warmth. It never came. I hadn't tested it after I installed it, and apparently the controller was faulty. Unfortunately, it didn't work the entire ride, but I never had the nerve to tell Dale.

I rechecked the bonus instructions to make sure I did everything correctly. The bonus was only available during daylight hours. Pulling into the visitors' parking lot an hour before sunrise, I decided to take advantage of my early arrival and lay my head on the soft bag attached to the gas tank of the RT. I struggled to stay warm, shivering uncontrollably. I had never been so cold in my life.

Unable to sleep, I was relieved when the sun finally came up. I stiffly climbed off the bike, pulled the rally pack out of the trunk, and reviewed the description one more time. I didn't want to come this far only to mess it up.

Mt. St. Helens National Volcanic Monument   400 points Available   DAYLIGHT HOURS!

Windy Ridge — Washington

Ride to the end of Forest Service Road 99 located inside Mt. St. Helens National Volcanic Monument on the EAST side of the park and take a picture of Spirit Lake OR the visitor amphitheater (this is a very small amphitheater with seating for just a few people) OR the "Windy Ridge View Point" sign OR the road closed sign at the end of the road in the park. *Your ID flag must be in the photo!*

NOTE: While you maybe able to ride into the park at night, we will not accept your photo unless taken during daylight hours.

Mt. St. Helens NVM is located in southwestern Washington State to the northeast of Portland, Oregon. The end of the road on the EAST side of Mt. St. Helens is located approximately twenty miles west from the intersection of Forest Road 25 and Forest Road 99 on the east side of Mt. St. Helens. There are several routes possible to the EAST side of Mt. St. Helens (all roads are paved). Once in the immediate area, the state of Washington has done a good job marking different routes up to the mountain.

WARNING: If you do not understand where to go, please see the rally master!

Time: _____ Odometer: _____ Code: ST

I filled in the required information, took my photo, and doubled checked to make sure it had all the necessary elements. I put everything back into its proper place, got back on the bike, and headed back off the mountain as quickly as possible to thaw out.

Rallying was turning out to be much harder than I anticipated. The details of the paperwork, the extremes of cold, and the exact timing required all added to the challenge. But rallying was also more fun than I had expected. I enjoyed the mental exercise of bonus hunting, seeing roads I might otherwise have missed, and the fun of knowing others were out there doing the same thing.

The second leg of the Rally continued the poison theme, with routes wandering through the country, all ultimately arriving in Maine. While the total points available by going north were higher, the route south was more appealing. I was not alone in my decision; the majority of the riders chose the same option, although it was rare to see another rider despite targeting the same bonuses. Different riding styles, rest and food stops, and the time it took to complete tasks separated us. Opting for a single, high point stop, a 'drop by and visit 1995 Rally veteran Ron Ayres at his home in Texas' bonus, I was soon on my way to Maine.

In the Leg Three rally pack, I noticed a huge bonus that required a return to New York before heading west to Ojai. Most of the leaders who were in serious contention for the top ten finishing spots opted to endure riding north once again on Interstate 95, knowing the points they would get would be worth the effort. However, remembering my goal to simply finish, I chose an alternate route, and took off toward the south before planning to head west. I picked up my first bonus—Perdido Beach in Alabama—then aimed for the Murrah Building in Oklahoma City, site of the domestic terrorist bombing in 1995.

~

"Mike, I'm having some problems with the bike," I said into the gas station phone. "I think it's a broken alternator belt. I just called the nearest BMW dealer and they've called a tow truck. I may be out of the Rally; I'll keep you posted."

Only minutes before I'd been flying along the interstate, well above the posted speed limit, actually hoping to be noticed by a police officer. I had been trying to escape an 'Easy Rider' wannabe in a Toyota pickup who'd been riding my tail, harassing me, and getting close enough to nearly push me off the road. The one time I wanted a cop none were to be found. I spied a gasoline station and checked my rearview mirrors to make sure the pickup was too far away to see me turn, then pulled into the driveway and hid the bike behind the pump. Watching the Toyota barrel by, I glanced down and noticed the red warning light indicating my alternator wasn't working. I located a BMW dealer and limped into the shop.

Luck was on my side. The owner called in a mechanic on his day off, cannibalized the showroom RT for parts, serviced the bike, and even washed it for me. Deeply appreciative of his efforts, I was ecstatic to be moving again. I called Mike to let him know I was still in the Rally.

"Where are you?" Mike queried.

"Oklahoma City," I replied, as if stating the obvious.

"What! You're supposed to be nearly to Ojai by now!" I could feel his head shaking through the phone lines. "You've got the bike working, now just get back here."

Ignoring Mike's advice to simply head to the finish, I picked up one last bonus, Meteor Crater near Flagstaff, Arizona, then pointed the bike toward Ojai. I made it with time to spare and took advantage of the time before the finisher's banquet to check in, take a long shower, and lie down for a nap. I hadn't been out of my riding suit in ten days, nor had I showered or shaved. At one food stop I mistakenly squirted ketchup onto my hands instead of on my French fries, causing more than one patron to politely move away from me.

Just as I nodded off, the phone rang.

Who could it be? Who besides Patti even knew I was there? I wondered as I picked it up. It turned out my mission to publicize Rotary had been successful; a local club wanted me to come speak at their program at noon; my hoped-for six hours of sleep was now cut to less than two. Despite my exhaustion, I obliged.

I sat with the others at the finisher's banquet, listening as names were called and riders went to the dais to receive their plaques and certificates. As predicted, the first place finisher, George Barnes, had gone to the White Plains, New York, bonus.

Calling names from lowest points to highest, I was pleased to learn I had achieved Bronze status, riding 10,419 miles and earning 24,457 points over the eleven days, 11,457 points more than if I had simply ridden checkpoint to checkpoint. While falling short of my own goal of riding 13,000 miles, I achieved my greater goal of bringing awareness to PolioPlus, particularly among the long-distance riding community. I also learned that the Iron Butt Rally was much more than 'sit here, twist that;' it was a thinking person's game, and I knew, if given the chance, I wanted to ride it again.

2000

The World Health Organization Western Pacific Region is certified polio-free. A record 550 million children, almost one-tenth of the world's population, receive the oral polio vaccine.

CHAPTER 18

As much as I loved riding, I was having a hard time pretending I was healthy and not in constant pain. The respite from my symptoms appeared to be over. The Rally had taken a toll, and it was becoming increasingly difficult for me to ignore the aching joints, muscle tension, and the struggle to get comfortable. I spent hours talking with Patti about what to do, and for the first time since my Post Polio diagnosis, thought about giving up motorcycling. My long distance rides had brought attention to Rotary's work with PolioPlus, but the wear and tear on me was causing genuine damage. Besides, the work was taking place a world away, and while I knew it was important, it still felt abstract.

"If you ever get an opportunity to go with Rotary on an International Immunization Day, I highly recommend you take advantage and go," Cliff Dochterman tossed out offhandedly at his Moraga Rotary club's weekly meeting where I had been invited to be the program speaker. Challenging me to look at what I might contribute as well as what I might learn, I was uncharacteristically reluctant. My fatigue and pain, both realities I was dealing with, were already causing me to question riding; why would I want to go to a foreign country and exhaust myself further? But other, louder voices also played in my head.

I've never been to the third world; what if I can't hack it?

What if I end up like Mother Teresa and never come back?

I feel bad for the people there, but why should I suffer just because I was born into more fortunate circumstances? Besides, I don't think I have much to offer.

My rides have done a lot already to raise awareness. I can keep up my public speaking and help that way.

My arguments were endless, and as I listened to them in my head, I heard a litany of excuses. Was I really afraid to go? I'd never avoided anything before, why was I trying to duck out now?

This is ridiculous. Get over yourself and go out and prove to yourself you can do this!

I was uncomfortable with the idea of going, yet I was more uncomfortable with the idea of quitting something before even trying. It was time to stretch beyond the familiar. I debated with myself until I was tired of my own voice.

I called Cliff. "You win. I'll sign up." He, of course, had never doubted I'd go.

"It looks like I'll be going to Ghana," I told Patti. I would be joining a group of ninety-two Rotarians from North America on a cultural journey, promoting the organization to young, potential Rotarians and functioning as observers on Immunization Day. Actually held over three days, thousands of volunteers from around the globe descend on the country, attempting to immunize over eight million children, providing lifetime protection against the dread disease.

"Please exit the airplane to the front, go down the steps and across the tarmac into the terminal where you will go through immigration. Do not take any photos inside the airport. It is against the law," our flight attendant announced, giving us our last minute instructions. As I watched the ground crew approach with the stairs, the airplane door opened and a sudden wave of unbearable humidity washed over me—my first taste of Ghana.

I stepped into the blinding sunlight and made my way down the metal stairway as the suffocating heat radiated off the asphalt. Once in the terminal, uniformed men carrying UZIs surrounded us, eyeing us with suspicion. But rather than reassuring me with their presence, I felt unnerved. The walls, barren of any décor, matched the room. Makeshift tables served as customs stations. Waiting in line, and wanting to capture every part of my experience, I pulled my camera near my waist.

'Click, click, click.' I snapped a few pictures, praying no one would notice and I would not end up spending the week in prison.

'Rotary International,' the bus driver's sign beckoned. I joined others from my flight and followed him outside.

"We will be driving through Accra to the coast, where you will be staying," he announced as we boarded. Closing the doors and starting the engine, I heard the defroster start up. The humidity, combined with the bus full of bodies, pressed in on us, fogging all the windows. When we arrived in the city, the smells and colors permeated my senses; I noticed the boarded-up buildings and the makeshift store fronts fashioned from the discarded carcasses of old metal shipping containers. People were everywhere, crowding the potholed streets and dirt sidewalks. Known as the Gold Coast during its British colonial days, and once one of the wealthiest countries in Africa, it was now one of the poorest. While gold has been its main export, and it is currently Africa's second largest gold producer, the coveted mineral provides wealth to a only a small fraction of the country, leaving most Ghanaians in poverty. Many of the best and brightest students leave as soon as they are able, never to return.

The city slowly gave way to increasingly tropical vegetation, and once at our hotel, we were surrounded by an equatorial paradise. Crystal clear ocean, luxurious buildings, and friendly staff greeted us. Having heard stories of dysentery from other third world travellers, I opted to avoid drinking water in all forms, including ice. Beer seemed like a safe alternative, and became my drink of choice for all my meals.

The first morning breakfast buffet on the dining veranda was stunning: fresh fruits, eggs, breads and a giant bowl of warm, inviting bacon. I filled my plate and savored each bite. On the second day, I noticed the bowl of bacon had not been changed, and by the time our week was finished, that same bacon, now rancid, was still in the bowl. I stuck with the fruit.

Buses arrived at our resort each day to take us to local tourist attractions and Rotary events. Knowing I wanted a more intimate experience than group tours on an air-conditioned bus, I hired a local driver and paid him the US equivalent of fourteen dollars a day to take me to places off the beaten track. Twenty minutes outside Accra we were in a different world, one filled with square dug ditches along the road and human feces everywhere, no sewers or running water to be found in any of the small compounds we passed. The stench of raw sewage was overwhelming, gagging me at every stop. Racks of fish, drying next to open cesspools, added to the smell. Yet the villagers were immaculately clean; they bathed daily, brushed their teeth with sticks and washed their clothes frequently, often carrying water long distances to accomplish their chores.

Cars far outnumbered motorbikes. My driver explained that anyone who owned a car and registered it as a taxi received numerous discounts on fees and taxes, so everyone considered their personal cars as taxis. The motorcycles I did see were jammed with people, animals, and baskets, hanging from every conceivable surface. I passed a sign for a BMW repair shop tacked up on the trunk of a giant tree, the alleged mechanics surrounded by broken down and rusted bikes. One was examining the engine of a particularly ancient machine while the other two supervised, hands and arms gesticulating wildly as they offered their opinions.

We visited small fishing villages where I watched as fishermen paddled up to a half mile out to sea in thirty to forty foot hollowed logs, a rope stretching from stern to shore. My guide explained they'd remain at sea until the boats were filled with fish, at which point young boys would haul them back to the beach.

"You give me 5,000 Cedi," the aged grandmother insisted, sitting next to a rack of drying fish. I calculated the exchange rate in my head: about seventeen cents US. I'd already planned to offer something, but was curious about her demand for payment.

"Why?" I replied.

"You take my picture, you pay me," she said, stubbornly.

"But I'm not taking your picture, I'm taking a picture of the fish," I corrected her.

"Yes, but if I not here, fish not here. You pay me," she grinned.

Chuckling at her logic, I happily paid.

We drove by several walled compounds and stopped to visit a few. Each compound, a concrete or mud structure perhaps 1,000 square feet in size, housed a large extended family in several huts. Each hut was filled with tiered bunks for sleeping, while most other activities commenced outside. Some had boards for the villagers to walk on, others merely paths between the open sewers. Able to speak several of the local dialects, my driver acted as interpreter.

"When the rainy season comes, sometimes our houses wash away and we are forced to rebuild everything." My early years on the road in our trailer felt like first class travel by comparison. It was hard to imagine such a precarious existence.

The roads, all in various states of disrepair, switched frequently from paved to dirt. Occasionally I saw groups of Ghanaians, having caught a bush rat, antelope, or monkey, standing around a fire. They'd gut their prize, stretch the carcass across a wooden frame and hold it over the flames until it was fully cooked, then scrape the meat from the skin. My driver offered to stop several times, and I had the opportunity to sample bites of several different animals, all of which had a slightly gamey flavor. The monkey, in particular, tasted extremely stringy. Glad for the experience, I doubted I'd ever want to eat any of the animals again.

Joining my fellow volunteers for an organized gathering one day, we were shepherded into a huge amphitheater for a meeting of the top Ghanaian Rotarians. The president of Ghana welcomed us warmly and praised us for our efforts on behalf of the children. Before going onstage to give my own speech, we listened to various others including one by Roger Moore of James Bond fame, who spoke on behalf of UNICEF.

Most Ghanaians, having never owned or seen a television, had heard that a famous person was in the country. As a foreigner with my own chauffeur, locals saw me and assumed I was the famous actor, waving and shouting "Roger Moore, Roger Moore!"

"Sure, sure, I'm James Bond!" I waved back, laughing.

As a group, we also visited Elmina Castle, the central processing point for the North American slave trade. We walked through the historic site, learned the history of the building and heard stories of abuse and servitude, where Africans had been captured and brought to the castle to be sold for shipment abroad. Stepping into the aptly named Death Chamber, a once airtight room used to punish 'problem' prisoners where so many had died, I could sense their presence still, two hundred years later. At the Gate of No Return, I felt an overwhelming sadness for those who suffered, forced to leave behind all they knew and loved.

Throughout the countryside, signs of polio were everywhere. Children, legs misshapen and immobile, crawled to the local garbage dumps to forage, looking for discarded junk to re-sell on street corners. Others hawked bags of water, hoping to attract a few pennies from tourists in the oppressive heat. Walking along the sidewalks we often had to weave between beggars, legs tucked uselessly underneath them, hands out in silent pleas for any help. Nicknamed crawlers by Dr. Joe Serra, who performed numerous surgeries on children with polio in Malawi more than twenty-five years ago, the name had stuck.

Flyers were put out weeks in advance of Immunization Day, all in different colors. It was a fun game among the local children to see how many colors they could collect. In the process, the word was spread and most parents were excited to bring their babies and young children for their vaccines. Loudspeakers broadcast our arrival, clearly announcing when to show up. We approached each compound, knocked on the wooden entry, and after explaining who we were, stood back as the doors opened and we were welcomed inside.

Working with a small group of Rotarians, we moved from compound to compound, setting up our workstation on benches, the vials of vaccines safely kept in coolers until needed. Mothers lined up patiently as their children surrounded us, eager to see the foreign strangers up close.

At one compound, I made my way up to the gate, which was barricaded, an unexpected complication. Pounding on the wooden boards, a tiny hole in the door slid open and the local Imam glared at me, his look conveying pure hatred. Accustomed to the enthusiastic greetings we had received at other villages, the Imam's cold glare was a shock. Even I could understand his meaning: he had no intention of letting in westerners or their voodoo medicine to poison his people.

His eyes, moving from the pale skin of my face, past my well-developed torso, settled quietly on my damaged legs—braces poking from under my pant legs—and the crutches in my hands. I saw a brief flicker of willingness to hear me out. I seized my one chance to change his mind.

"We want to save your children. We want to help. The medicine is safe. To prove it isn't poison, I will take two drops from every vial myself. I will promise you with my life that we mean no harm."

He slammed the panel shut. I had failed. I waited for what seemed like an eternity in the sweltering heat, angry and confused.

Just then, the door swung open, and I was staring directly at the Imam, the men of the village behind him in a show of force. Our tiny group of volunteers wouldn't stand a chance of survival if they came at us.

"I will watch you closely. You will take a taste from every new box. I will choose the vial in case you are tricking me."

Bowing slightly and thanking him, I breathed deeply once again. We were going inside. His henchmen followed our every move, their distrust evident in their stares.

A young mother approached our group and gently handed her baby girl to me. Opening the vial, I began to pry apart her tiny mouth, prepared for the screams that often followed the sour tasting medicine. I'd felt a tugging on my pant leg for several minutes and had done my best to ignore it, but it grew increasingly insistent. Unable to shake it off, I finally glanced down, and was met by huge brown eyes and clear white teeth. My gaze continued down to his shriveled legs tangled in the dirt. A crawler.

"Thank you, mister, for saving my sister so she doesn't get what I've got," he spoke directly to me in his flawless English.

Tears immediately sprang to my eyes. I wiped them with my arm and breathed deeply to regain my composure. I looked down at him. His face radiated calmness and compassion, and he smiled up at me.

"You're welcome," I said, barely able to get the words out. "You're welcome."

People always assumed my efforts on behalf of polio were because of my own experience, yet that was never my motivation. I volunteered because it was important to Rotary and our club. My life was good; my memories of polio were distant. My childhood had been filled with love and opportunity, adventure and education; nothing had stopped me from doing what I wanted to do. Looking into that young man's eyes, I came face to face with what it meant to have polio in a developing nation: a life of begging, of living in the shadows, without work and often without family. I felt punched in the gut. The work we were doing mattered; we were affecting real lives, real people.

Back in the hotel, I called Patti, crying. "I can't give up, I have to keep going. I may be in pain, but it's nothing compared to what these kids live with."

The fight to eradicate polio had just become personal.

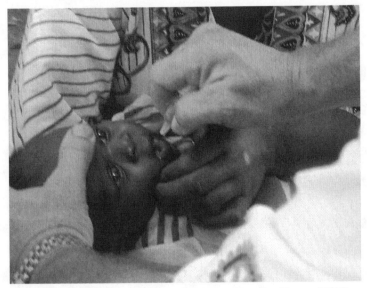
Delivering magic drops, one child at a time, in Ghana (2000)

Polio creates lifelong challenges for its victims (Ghana, 2000)

2002

The World Health Organization European Region
is certified polio-free.

CHAPTER 19

On the way home from Ghana, the images of the children depending on Rotary for their very lives—and by extension, me—kept replaying in my mind. Before the trip, I'd been considering stopping my rides, no longer sure the pain and fatigue in my body was worth whatever good I might be doing. But now I realized whatever discomforts I had were miniscule compared to the problems we were trying to alleviate. What right did I have to complain when I slept in a warm bed with a full belly, living a life surrounded by loving family and numerous friends? Surely I was willing to be uncomfortable for the greater good?

If I was completely honest, I had to admit that—for the most part—the motivations for my PolioPlus rides in the past were personal. They brought attention to the work of Rotary, but, in reality, I had been doing them as much for my own enjoyment as for PolioPlus. I relished the freedom of riding, of taking time off work and travelling, and sharing in the camaraderie of the people I met. This time something really had changed; I felt the shift deeply. Sitting with that young man I had become a Rotarian; I was no longer simply a member of Rotary. Now I felt like a soldier in a battle for the very lives of those children. I was genuinely concerned about the lives of others I might never actually meet.

I now knew, no matter my level of discomfort, the rides for awareness would continue, and I contemplated my next steps. At an earlier Rotary International convention someone had pinned a koala on my jacket, remarking 'we expect you to bring this back to Australia.' Perhaps it was time to make good on his invitation. The perimeter of the continent, along with a tour of the capitals of each state, would make a perfect ride. I asked two of my buddies to join me—Bill McKenna, past president of the Augusta, Maine, Rotary club, and Walter Helm, from the Point West Rotary club in Sacramento— and both jumped at the chance. A third friend, Jon Green, the webmaster for the PolioPlus.org website, offered to drive a support truck. A plan began taking shape.

For twelve hundred dollars each way, I arranged for a shipping company to transport my motorcycle and sidecar, and packed it carefully for its six-week sea voyage. Not needing the specialized equipment I required, Bill and Walter would rent bikes once we landed. We finalized our plans before flying halfway across the world, and I bid farewell to Patti, who would be joining me for a two-week vacation once we finished the ride.

~

I stood in the shipyard and watched, horrified, as the forklift carrying cargo to shore tilted forward and the crate containing my bike dropped with a thud on the pavement. The wood splintered with a sharp crack, and through the gaping holes I saw that despite the tethers I'd put in place to hold everything securely, my bike and sidecar had fallen. Prying open the box, it was obvious the windshield was shattered, but remarkably the other damage, although extensive, was primarily cosmetic. Fortunately I had packed a spare screen, and I was able to replace the broken one before we headed out.

Prior to our trip, Jon and I were in frequent contact with Tony Moyle, the founder of the International Federation of Motorcycling Rotarians. Through Tony, we were able to arrange home stays for us in many of the towns we visited, which provided a personal opportunity to talk to locals about Rotary. We spent several hours comparing clubs in Australia Rotary to Rotary in the United States with many of our hosts.

As with my previous rides, speaking engagements and meetings with local dignitaries were arranged through various Rotary groups, as were tours of the area's highlights. Sitting next to the Secretary of the Interior at a fundraising event, I turned to ask what to me was an obvious question before starting into the outback.

"What critters do I need to watch for? Which ones are dangerous?" I inquired.

Looking at me like I had lost my mind, she replied slowly, "Why, mate, they're all dangerous!"

Somewhere in the Northern Territory we stopped for the night at a lush lakeside resort. As I headed out for a walk, I inquired about the possibility of crocodiles.

"No worries, mate. They haven't found a way to get past the dam yet," the hotelier assured me.

Along the shore, I walked across a tangle of tree roots, not realizing how far into the water they stretched. My crutch slipped into a gap between two branches, and I felt it flutter; whatever I was poking wasn't a tree, it was alive. Scrambling back to solid ground, I confronted the owner.

"You said there were no crocs here," I said, demanding an explanation.

"Right, mate, we don't have crocs, only Johnsons," he answered calmly.

"What are they?" I insisted.

"Johnson crocodiles," he replied, as if it was completely obvious.

"How big do they get?" I inquired.

"Oh, only three or four meters," he smiled.

Apparently Johnsons weren't big enough in his mind to qualify as crocs. I stayed clear of the water the remainder of our trip.

On the outskirts of Hobart, Tasmania, I felt the bike suddenly lurch. "No, no! Not again!" I yelled. "What's broken this time?" Just then the axle on the sidecar snapped, sending the wheel sailing. I skidded to a stop, and watched as it landed twenty feet up a nearby tree.

Bill pulled up beside me. "My wheel is up in that tree over there. Think you can get it down?" We both stood and looked for a moment before he nodded.

He walked back a ways and found the axle on the side of the road. "I have Margaret Weyle-Willett's number. Let me ring her up and see if she can help us out." Margaret, a Rotarian we'd met in Melbourne, answered immediately.

"The Parilla dealer is the motorcycle shop closest to you. I'll get a tow truck out there and arrange for the dealer to stay open until he can bring you in. I'll get back to you as soon as I can." Within twenty minutes the phone rang. "All done. They should be there shortly."

Scheduled for a speaking engagement in only a couple of hours, I hitched a ride from the tow truck driver to the Claremont Rotary Club. Still in my motorcycling gear, in my haste, I'd forgotten not only a change of clothes but also a belt for my riding pants. I struggled to hold myself together while trying to walk at the same time.

"You can't go in like that," the driver commented. "There's a shop on the way. You need to get something a bit more decent. Can't be worrying about your pants falling down while you're speaking."

"It's on me, mate," he insisted when I pulled my wallet out to pay for my new ensemble. "Won't take a dime off you." He also wouldn't accept anything for the tow of over 120 kilometers. "It's all for polio," was his final comment.

"You have to at least let me pay something." I had to force him to take fifty Australian dollars for the gas.

While we waited for a new axle to be machined and installed, Bill and I had time to squeeze in an interview with the local ABC radio affiliate and a second Rotary club. By the time we boarded the ferry back to the mainland, we were approached by several passengers who had heard our interviews. Word was spreading.

I'd noticed some weakness in my right shoulder before the trip, and as the ride progressed, it was becoming more pronounced. Lifting my arm to reach the handlebars required more effort than I could manage, forcing me to manually place it on the grip with my other hand. In one of my phone calls home I mentioned it to Patti.

"I need you to set up an appointment with the orthopedist for when I get back. This shoulder is getting worse, and I'm guessing it's going to need some serious repair work. I'm sure I can still finish the ride," I hastened to add, not sure if I was reassuring her or me.

In many of the smaller villages townspeople often blocked our way, hoping to meet us and get an interview for their paper. The process was repeated frequently as the media, catching wind of our ride, began showing up at many of the venues where we were appearing. People's generosity greeted us wherever we went. Hotel rooms, motorcycle repairs, homemade dinners, anything we needed was often offered before we had a chance to ask.

Caught in a huge rainstorm, we decided to stay put for the night en route from Albany to Perth. Looking for a room, a man in the bar sent Bill to the office at the far end of the hotel. A newcomer to Australian humor, he wasn't quite prepared when a woman, old enough to be his grandmother, opened the door at his knock. Completely nude, she seemed unfazed at his arrival.

"So, uh, where do I register?" he stuttered. "Isn't this the front desk?"

"Sure it is, mate. Come on in," she purred.

"I think I've been had," he chuckled as he turned around and returned to the bar.

"You're a good sport, mate. Ever come back to these parts, we'll stand you a round." The group had a hearty laugh at his expense, with Bill perhaps laughing the loudest.

Rather than divide every bill by four, we kept things simple by rotating who paid for meals and gas. Jon had no compunction about ordering a huge meal when someone else was buying, and somehow managed to find the cheapest restaurants when it was his turn to pick up the tab. The van, requiring premium gas, was filled with regular when his card was charged. Periodically I threatened to send him home if he didn't cough up his fair share.

"Did someone leave this credit card?" the girl yelled, running out of the diner.

"Oh, man, thanks, it's mine." I caught her before she could reach Jon, the rightful owner. Then, without mentioning to Jon, I said, "I'm paying with this card." Bill, Walter, and I ordered the best food and premium gas, enjoying our little joke.

Jon finally noticed his card was missing. "Damn, I need to

cancel my card. I lost it somewhere along the way."

"No need to call anyone, Jon, I've got your card right here. Unbeknownst to you, you've been very generous these last few days, and we all appreciate your finally stepping up. Remember that time I took you out and you brought three of your friends and ordered the most expensive items on the menu? You know how you always go all out when the rest of us are paying? Well, buddy, this is payback!"

"You SOBs!" he shouted, although his laughter indicated he knew he probably deserved the punishment.

~

In the Northern Territory, we cranked up our speed. The open roads and empty expanses were irresistible, and with no one around, it felt perfectly safe. I noticed what appeared to be gumball lights in the distance and assumed I was seeing things, but I slowed down nonetheless. As Walter and Bill flew past me, I watched the local law enforcement officer's light bar flash.

Catching up with them, I pulled over, grabbed my crutches and hopped off the bike, and walked over to join the conversation.

"I'm not going to write you a ticket, but the speed limit is 110 kilometers here. You were well over that." The officer looked at the group of us.

"I don't know why you pulled us over in any case," Bill explained. "Seems perfectly safe out here. We can see in every direction."

"Well, mate, you didn't see me then, did you?" he replied. For once, Bill had no answer.

About fifty miles outside of Hughenden, Queensland, my bike started making noises that sounded suspiciously like a dying transmission. Pulling to the side of the road, the four of us stood around and discussed our options.

With no one around, we hadn't seen a car in ages, and it was too hot to leave me while they rode on ahead, we came to the same conclusions: we needed to find a way to haul it ourselves. We attached a rope from Walter's bike to mine and towed it into town.

"Well, this isn't good," I sighed, leaning against my bike. "Broken bike, nine hundred miles northwest of Brisbane, and not a repair shop of any kind to be found." Hughenden was too small an outpost to provide any source of relief. "This looks like the end of the road for my ride. I'll get the bike towed back to Brisbane for the return home, and we can meet up in Cairns like we planned. No sense you guys cutting short your ride." Reluctantly, everyone agreed.

The bike safely loaded on the tow truck, Jon and I drove the van to Cairns where Patti and the other wives greeted us. Once Walter and Bill arrived, we spent the next two weeks sightseeing before returning to Brisbane, where I was reunited with my still broken bike that was on display during the Rotary International Convention.

We assessed the impact of our journey. A year and a half prior to our trip Rotary had announced a need to raise eighty million dollars. At the convention in Brisbane, it was announced they had over eighty-eight million in cash and pledges. We had set out to help local Rotarians increase awareness about the final push to eradicate polio. Our trip was one small contribution to that success.

After dropping off the bike at the Morgan and Wacker motorcycle service department for repair, I made final shipping arrangements before Patti and I flew home to California. The price for the return mysteriously increased to seven thousand dollars from the original twelve hundred. Held hostage by the shipping company that knew I had no other options for getting the bike home, I had no choice but to pay. But when I returned home, I was pleasantly surprised to find a check from insurance for the damages caused by the careless unloading of my bike at the start of my trip... for exactly seven thousand dollars.

~

My shoulder had become nearly useless, and the pain was intense every time I tried to lift my arm, so once back in the States, I met with the orthopedist who recommended an MRI. I relaxed on the small foam pad while the attendant helped me adjust my headphones and placed my arms by my sides. As the bed lifted and moved into the machine, I closed my eyes, hopeful the results would clarify what needed repair and I could get on with my life.

Curious to see what the device looked like from inside, I opened my eyes. "Get me out NOW!" I screamed. The sides were closing in on me and I couldn't move. "GET ME OUT!"

I was experiencing a full-blown panic attack, sweat soaking my clothes, my heart racing uncontrollably, and my fingernails digging into my palms. The attendant rushed into the room and yanked the bed out from the tunnel where I had been enclosed. I ripped off my headphones, and, shaking from head to toe, tried to catch my breath.

"I have never, ever, felt so trapped. I thought I was going to die!" The words came out in gasps. I was stunned by the vehemence of my response.

"We've seen this before," the attendant reassured me with his calm, measured voice. "Sometimes the close confines of the MRI tube triggers old memories, and sometimes people just don't like small spaces."

"I don't remember having a fear of small spaces; I've never been uncomfortable in elevators or working in cramped conditions." As I wiped my face with a towel the attendant gave me, my breathing slowly returned to normal. Unable to figure out the intensity of my reaction, I thought about what he had said. 'Old memories.' Then it hit me.

"Oh my god, it's the iron lung. I don't have any memory of it, but my mother told me I was in one off and on during my years in the hospital. Apparently my body remembers even though I can't. I've never felt this panicked before. All I felt was that I had to get out, that my life depended on it." Making sense of my experience helped me calm down.

"Let's get this over with," I said, focusing on each breath to distract me from my thoughts. Forcing myself to contain my panic, not wanting to let it control my life, I lay back down on the bed and completed the test. My orthopedic surgeon and good friend, Dr. Guy Guilfoy, successfully repaired my right shoulder as well as my left shoulder a few years later.

Boy in Emerson respirator (Iron Lung) at Herman Keifer Hospital
in Detroit, Michigan. Joe Clark, photographer (1955)

The Australian team, left to right:
Bill McKenna, Walter Helm, me, John Greene (2003)

2003

After opposition to vaccinations from mullahs in Nigeria, cases triple, ultimately leading to a spread of polio from that country to West Africa.

CHAPTER 20

"Tell us you drained all the fluids from your bike and disconnected the battery," the attendant hinted as I rode the RT into the belly of the cargo plane destined for Hawaii.

"Why, yes, I drained all the fluids and disconnected the battery," I dutifully replied, as I turned off the key, picked up my crutches, and dismounted the bike.

"Alright then, it'll be waiting for you in Hilo," he cheerfully responded, checking the requisite box on the shipping form, apparently satisfied with my answer.

Following the successes of both my 48-30 and Trans-Canada rides, I planned to combine the two, visiting the lower forty-eight state and all nine Canadian provincial capitals, ending at Rotary's Centennial celebration in Chicago, Illinois, in June 2005. An offer from the Hawaiian Rotary to bring my bike, Patti, and me to the islands spurred my decision to make it a fifty-state ride, adding Alaska after the convention.

In Hilo, we were greeted by several local Rotary clubs. My rig, flown to Oahu and then barged to the Big Island, awaited me. Patti, on a rented Harley Sportster, and I took off on a counterclockwise tour, stopping at various locations to greet groups and sightsee. Our next stop, Maui, was a bit more complicated. Because of bureaucratic issues, my bike wasn't allowed to join us, so instead of riding, we toured the island in a Mustang convertible with an escort of Rotarians on motorcycles.

Prior to our invitation to Hawaii, I had been scheduled to speak at a Rotary gathering in Seattle for 500 incoming club presidents, so I arranged to fly over for a quick turnaround and meet up again with Patti in Kauai.

Unfortunately, my luggage opted to take a more circuitous trip and detoured through New Orleans, arriving in Seattle long after I had departed. The Doubletree Hotel scrambled and found me a highly starched, oversized, crisp white shirt and dated tie. I put them on and headed toward the ballroom. My friend, Dick Elixman, pulled me aside in the hallway just before I entered the room, excited to show me something.

"Bob, what's wrong with you?" Dick's words cut through my blank stare. "You're shaking; sweat's dripping off your forehead. What's going on?"

"It's the same feeling I had during the MRI; something's out to get me. My heart's racing and I can't breathe!"

I struggled to regain my composure in front of my fellow Rotarian as I stared at the fully functioning iron lung he'd brought me in to see, listening to it as it sucked air in and out of the giant chamber. In all the years I'd talked about polio, I still had no visual memory of being in one. Now I was face to face with the monster and felt sheer terror, clear that my body still remembered. The sight of the huge machine, the dreaded 'whoosh, whoosh' was all too overwhelming. All I could think of was escape.

"Dick, we have to move into the other room; I can't stand it, I have to go." For once, I walked away from something I feared. It evoked too many memories.

Taking several minutes to regain my composure, I entered the ballroom and after a brief introduction, climbed the steps to the stage. At the podium, I needed no notes. I looked out at the crowd and cleared my throat.

Hello fellow Rotarians,

First of all, I'd like to thank the Doubletree for the use of this shirt and tie while my clothes are off having a grand time visiting another city.

But what I really came here to talk about is polio. When I was nine-months-old, I was stricken with the disease and spent the next three plus years in the hospital... and as I was reminded so vividly a few minutes ago, much of that time was in an iron lung...

Rotary got involved in the fight to eradicate polio in 1985...

I wasn't that involved in PolioPlus for years. I believe I was in denial about my own experience and had spent most of my life avoiding the stigma of having had polio...

In 1985 I was diagnosed with Post Polio Syndrome and given two years before I'd be in a wheelchair. The three neurologists who confirmed my diagnosis are all dead. I, on the other hand, went out, bought a motorcycle, and put seven thousand miles on it the first week after my diagnosis. I felt better and more alive than I had in years...

I have always hated being told I can't do something. People have thrown obstacles in my way, and instead of bemoaning my situation, I've spent my life finding ways to level the playing field. When told 'you can't,' I found a way to turn it into 'yes, I can.' It reminds me of the time Stevie Wonder met Tiger Woods.

"Hey, Tiger, we need to play golf together sometime," Stevie suggested.

"You can't play. You're blind!" Tiger responded, incredulous at the suggestion. "How can you possibly know where to hit the ball?"

"Well, when I need to make a shot down the fairway, my caddie moves to where I want it to go and shouts at me. I aim the ball where his voice is,"

Stevie explained.

"Okay, but how do you putt?" Tiger persisted.

"My caddie goes to the cup, gets down on the ground, and calls to me. I aim where his voice is," Stevie continued.

"Well, then, maybe we should play," Tiger declared.

"Tiger, I am offended by people repeatedly thinking I can't do something just because I am blind. If you want to play, we'll have to make it worth it. I will only play you if we bet $10,000 per hole."

"Well, that's a wild bet!" replied Tiger, assuming he'd easily win. "Sure, let's do it. When do you want to play?"

"Any night next week," smiled Stevie. "Let's say we tee off around midnight?"

Motorcycling is one of the ways I've leveled the playing field. Getting that first sidecar let me ride and compete as an equal. Motorcycling is also one of the ways I've been able to help Rotary.

My first tour, to the capitals of the lower forty-eight states, generated free publicity for our efforts to end polio. Subsequent rides have continued to spread the word. Feature stories, articles in publications such as the Washington Post...

I'm proud of bringing others into the fight that aren't part of Rotary. The California Highway Patrol has been a huge supporter... in fact, I've probably been escorted out of Sacramento more often than any other person. Everywhere I go the long-distance motorcycling community hands me checks for PolioPlus...

When I was a kid, my family went into San Francisco once a month to a fancy restaurant. My father and I had to wear ties, and my sister and I were expected to behave like proper children. Each time when we arrived, I noticed a man, a crawler, sitting on a short four-wheeled cart with a can filled with pencils. Taped to the outside of the can was a sign 'Pencils 2 – 25 cents.' I didn't need the pencils, but I always stopped to drop in a quarter. We never spoke until one night he stopped me.

"Hey, kid, come here, I want to talk to you," he called out as I passed.

"Yeah, I know, you want to know why I never take a pencil after all these years, right?" I turned to face him. I noticed the tag on the can was missing.

"No, that's not why," he replied. "I wanted to let you know the price has gone up to thirty-five cents." Laughing, I dug into my pocket for the additional dime.

Now what does that story have to do with Rotary? It's a reminder that the cost of providing vaccines does go up, and the longer we delay, the more we will spend. It's important we move forward, quickly and forcefully, to end this battle while the finish line is within our grasp.

Every delay means another child suffers from this preventable disease. Every delay means another otherwise productive person is shunted aside, often sentenced to a lifetime of begging.

"History will be kind to me because I will write it." Winston Churchill's well-known quote applies here. We have the opportunity to write new histories for these children, to help them become productive members of their families and their communities.

Before I end, I want to take a moment to share with you a very personal story about the war we are waging against this disease, a war that affects real people, real lives. I want to tell you about a young man in Ghana, a young man who cared only that his sister be spared the suffering he endured.

His face before me, I choked up. Memories of Ghana flooded my mind and for a moment I could not speak. Struggling to compose myself, I barely finished my story, wiping away the tears that I cannot stop from flowing when I speak about PolioPlus.

~

The luggage, my bike, Patti and I were reunited in Lihue, Kauai. We finished our Hawaiian ride with a Poker Run on Oahu, a one hundred and ten mile circuit of the island with one hundred other riders. Picking up a playing card from a deck at each of several stops, the person with the best poker hand takes the prize. Mine was not the best hand that day, but PolioPlus came out the clear winner.

Back on the mainland, I met up with Tony Hennessy, a fellow I'd met in Tasmania during my Australian ride. The plan was for him to join me for all but the Alaska portion of the trip. Remembering the ribbing I'd endured learning the customs down under, I was only too happy to repay, American style.

"It's important you understand a few of our rules, Tony," I shared as we finished the final packing of our bikes. "For example, it's a federal law that if you order a full meal at a restaurant, it's okay to leave food, but if you only order a side dish, you must clear your plate. It's a weird rule, to be sure, but for some reason, one that is strictly enforced."

Gullible and unfamiliar with America, Tony made sure to obey. Stopping one morning at a Cracker Barrel, we ordered breakfast. "I always loved the TV show *Alice Doesn't Live Here Anymore* and her famous line: 'Kiss my grits.' I just have to try grits once while I'm here," he shared with the waitress. "I'll have the eggs and bacon, and a side of grits, please."

After his first bite of the thick corn porridge on his plate, his face contorted with disgust.

"These are awful, mate! How does anyone eat this mess?" he implored. He tried every combination I suggested— with syrup, milk, and gravy onto small clumps—to no avail. Adding butter and jelly proved no better.

"Damn that law! I can't believe I have to clean this plate," he lamented, not realizing he need not have ordered the side, as his breakfast already came with the dreaded southern specialty.

"Yes, shame, isn't it." I bit the inside of my cheek to hold back my laughter at his plight. "And Cracker Barrel is known to be especially vigilant about it."

Two weeks later, he stormed out of his hotel room, gunning for me.

"You SOB! I just had breakfast at the restaurant downstairs, and they looked at me like I was a lunatic when I said something about side dishes. You bastard!"

"Sorry, mate. Simply payback for some of the tricks you Aussies played on me!" I laughed.

~

Approaching Texarkana, Texas, late one Sunday night, we noticed my rear tire was down to the wear bars and needed replacing before we could ride much further. With BMW shops closed on Sundays and Mondays, and auto stores not carrying bike tires, waiting until Tuesday would create serious delays in our schedule.

We sent a plea for help to the small online listserv for those who have finished an Iron Butt Rally, which was passed on to the much larger Long Distance Rider group. Within minutes, Bill Thweat, a rider several states away, found a tire in Dallas and offered to have it shipped overnight to Arkansas, our next destination.

We rode all night in pouring rain at speeds averaging thirty-five miles an hour to preserve what tread remained, and arrived at Little Rock BMW just as the owner and his mechanic pulled in to meet us on their day off. The dealer took a tire off a bike in the showroom, intending to replace it with the one Bill was sending as soon as it was delivered.

They noticed Tony's tire was almost as bald as mine, and changed his as well. Refusing payment, he gave each of us a new pair of gloves. Bill declined to let me reimburse him for any expenses, only allowing me to buy him a beer as a thank you the next time I saw him.

As we rode into Raleigh, North Carolina, I caught the attention of a local enforcement officer. Red lights flashing, he pulled me over while Tony cruised past me as if I were a total stranger.

Explaining my ride to the policeman, he offered to escort me to the capital where we found ourselves surrounded by over forty bikers honoring North Carolina's POWs/MIAs from the Vietnam era. We stopped to chat and exchange stories; they were quite impressed with our journey and our mission. Finally alone again, I asked Tony about his earlier actions into town.

"Hey, mate, if you were going to be hauled into jail I certainly didn't see a need for me to go with you." Apparently he'd been watching too many American TV shows and had a distorted view of the local police.

From Helena, Montana, to Boise, we opted to take back roads through Craters of the Moon National Park and Sun Valley. Cresting a hill, the weather changed suddenly from sixty-five degrees and clear to three inches of golf ball-sized hail pounding us through our gear.

With Tony in my sights as he rode behind me, I was attempting to slow down when I noticed his bike swerve, regain its upright position, and then slide out from under him. As he landed on his shoulder, his head bounced on the hard concrete.

I stopped as soon as I could in the ice-covered road, carefully turned my bike around, and came back to him just as a truck approached from the other direction.

"You okay?" I shouted. The truck driver jumped out and ran over to Tony, who was slowly sitting up. He removed his helmet and took a minute to assess the damages.

"Yeah, mate, I think I'm okay. Banged up a bit. Shoulder feels a bit off, but I think it's just bruised." He stood up and walked around. "Yeah, the shoulder's not quite right, but if we can get somewhere warm and dry you can tape it up for me, Bob." It helped that Tony was a physical therapist back in Australia.

We loaded his bike into the half empty truck, and I followed them into Boise. Arriving just in time for a scheduled speech, Tony came with me, but it was soon apparent he needed medical attention. The doctor at the local emergency room assessed the damage: Tony had separated the clavicle from his scapula. His riding trip in America had come to an end, just eight capitals short of our goal.

Glad to know he would quickly recover, I left him under the excellent care of local Rotarians Hal and Sue Ramsey, and continued on my own. Patti's BMW R1100RT, which Tony had borrowed, was shipped home to Folsom with only minor damage.

Tony flew to Davenport, Iowa, where we met up and said our goodbyes. Completing the ride solo with a visit to Juneau, Alaska, a month after the lower forty-eight, I had now been to every state in America on behalf of PolioPlus.

Before leaving home, I'd gathered three Rotary Centennial bells, commemorating the one hundredth anniversary of the founding of the organization. The bells disassemble into thirds, and taking a piece from each of the three, I made a single one that I carried on the entire trip.

At all the meetings I attended, the bell was rung each time a member came up and donated money to PolioPlus. At one meeting alone, sixteen hundred dollars was raised. Later, I placed the parts back into their original bells, giving one to the Rotary District Governor of Hawaii, the second to the District Governor of Sacramento, and kept the third one for myself as a memento of my ride.

CHAPTER 21

After successfully completing a second Iron Butt Rally in 2001, I had finally earned credibility within the long-distance riding community. Hoping to ride again in 2003, my sidecar broke, and despite feverish efforts to repair it in time for the start, I wasn't able to participate. Instead, with my father keeping me company on the trip, we drove in my car to Missoula, Montana, to greet riders as they finished the event. Happy for them, it was torturous nonetheless not to be riding myself.

Home again, I received a call from a friend wondering if I was interested in his support for PolioPlus. Tom Melchild, the Rallymaster for the Cal 24, wanted to include donations to a worthy cause along with registration for his event. Tom had been one of the few veteran riders who welcomed me, a rookie, into his circle, when I showed up for my first Iron Butt Rally. I had no prior rally experience, was driving a bike with a sidecar, and hadn't even documented any Iron Butt rides. Most participants chatted with friends or focused on last minute preparations. For some I was a curiosity, but primarily I was ignored.

Though I'd heard many stories of the event, I'd never ridden in his twenty-four hour rally across all corners of California. The Cal 24 had a strong history of supporting charities, but Tom had become dissatisfied with their most recent recipient. He wanted a partnership, not merely a place to send a check, and I was thrilled to have another venue to publicize the efforts of PolioPlus.

Each participant was required to donate a minimum of fifty dollars to Rotary as part of their entry fees. Tom contacted various vendors associated with long-distance riding, such as Garmin, the manufacturer of the GPS units most often used on motorcycles, and Aerostich/RiderWearHouse, makers of the Roadcrafter suit preferred by many riders. They generously donated prizes that Tom gave to whomever raised the most money for PolioPlus. Offering high bonus points to any rider who put a 'Goodbye Polio, Thanks Rotary' sticker on his or her bike ensured word was spread, and many of the entrants eagerly added them to the various assorted other stickers covering their saddlebags and fuel cells.

Tom kept to his word about wanting a true partnership, and put me to work helping with the rally. Checking in riders, assisting with technical inspections to ensure each bike met minimum standards, hiding in secret locations with a radar gun to keep riders honest, and speaking at the Finishers' Banquets were just a few of my assigned tasks.

Many riders who heard about PolioPlus for the first time through Tom's event have since become avid supporters. My solo efforts to raise awareness now multiplied throughout the country as a cadre of long-distance riders, bikes blazoned with bright yellow stickers, were taking the message with them on their travels.

I regained entry into the Iron Butt Rally 2005, and once more rode on behalf of PolioPlus, planning on it being my last IBR. The protests from my body, becoming increasingly louder and louder, begged me to quit. The recent death of a well-known and well-respected member of the Iron Butt family, Ron Smith, was especially poignant for me. I'd noticed the auxiliary fuel cell on his bike at a gathering of riders in Seattle in 2004. I discovered he custom-made the cells for other riders, and talked with him about making one for me, but heard nothing more.

"Ron made you a fuel cell; it was the last one he made before he died. It's here for you." Ron's friend, Joe Zulaski, was on the other end of the line. "You know he was a huge supporter of Rotary's efforts to eradicate polio, and I want to raise enough money in his name to earn a posthumous Paul Harris Fellowship Award to give to his wife." Joe raised the required thousand dollars and arranged a gathering of long-distance riders. I rode up to Seattle to celebrate, presenting Ron's wife with the plaque.

My efforts to raise awareness of PolioPlus were making significant inroads in the long-distance community, greatly aided by the support of Tom and the Cal 24. When I arrived in Denver for the start of the Rally, riders greeted me and handed over checks made out to Rotary. This became a common occurrence whenever I ran into someone I knew or who had heard of me and/or my rides. 'Stop Polio Now' and 'Goodbye Polio, Thanks Rotary' stickers were visible on many of the bikes in the parking lot.

That year the Rally started and ended in the Mile High City, with two checkpoints: one at the start hotel, and one in Maine. John Bolin, a friend of Ron's, brought the fuel cell to Denver, and I met up with him outside the hotel. Dedicating part of my ride in Ron's memory, I attached the tank to my bike. By now familiar with the pre-rally preparations, I visited with friends, made sure my bike was ready, and waited with the others for the start of the ride.

~

What the hell? The headlights were approaching so rapidly they surprised me on the otherwise straight, empty road. *It must be going well over a hundred!* The van suddenly swerved directly in front of me and careened off the road. It spun wildly and flipped end over end before flying through the air, landing twenty yards behind me in a ditch. I screeched to a stop and made a tight U-turn, maneuvering my bike to the edge of the slope. Grabbing my crutches, I climbed down to the wreckage. The van doors had popped open on impact, and body parts and pieces of steel were everywhere, the exposed surfaces covered in bright red. I called 911, then began searching frantically for anyone who might have survived.

I stayed until emergency crews arrived, and learned that the van's driver, smuggling Mexican nationals across the border, had crammed men into any corner available. I struggled for miles to rid my mind of the images of crushed bodies, and kept trying to bring my attention back to the rally. Pictures flashing through my mind distracted me from driving, and I didn't want to end up a statistic myself. I heard later that only four of the passengers survived.

Returning to the Denver checkpoint, I was surprised to see a huge gash on my leg covered with dried blood when I stripped off my gear to shower. In my rush to help the victims I never felt the steel slash my thigh above my brace. I covered it with bandages from my first aid kit and climbed into bed, exhausted. Managing a few hours sleep interspersed with nightmares, I woke up in time to go downstairs for the distribution of the next leg's bonuses.

No longer a neophyte rallyist, I attempted more bonuses, wanting to improve my personal performance. Pulling up to the plaque, monument, building, or other site to take the required photo, I stopped the bike and swung my right leg over the seat. I then pulled my left leg off the foot peg and placed it on the ground, locking the brace into its straight position. With a crutch in each arm, I stood, walked to the back of the bike, and opened the top box to get my camera and rally flag. I re-read the instructions in the rally pack once more to ensure I took the correct photo, and walked to the bonus, hoping it wasn't too far or the ground too challenging. Finding a place to drape or hang my flag, I retreated far enough to capture all the required elements in the picture, knowing one small mistake could disqualify the entire bonus. Then

I reversed the procedure; double-checked everything before looking at my list for my next stop, entered the coordinates for the next bonus into my GPS, and took off. Most riders have perfected their bonus stops to barely a minute; I was happy if I was back on the bike in ten. The process, repeated with each gas, food or rest break, added up over the course of the eleven-day rally, taking valuable time away from riding.

By the second day of Leg Three my leg was red, swollen, and in need of attention. Soap and water turned out to be inefficient in preventing an infection in the cut I'd received while attending to the accident victims. I stopped at a pharmacy for an antibiotic cream, hoping it would tide me over until the finish. Adding to my concerns was a slipping clutch on the RT. At first I only had to avoid fifth gear, but as the miles piled on I had to give up on fourth. Finally reduced to only three gears, I spent nineteen hours riding at a top speed of thirty, hugging the edge of the road with my hazard lights flashing as I limped to the finish line in Denver. I had hoped for an improvement in the standings from the Bronze category in 1999, but after all that had occurred I was happy to simply qualify as a Finisher.

A fellow rider, Norm Babcock, offered to trailer my bike to Lawrence, Kansas, after Paul Glaves offered to repair the damaged clutch. My leg, finally on the mend, was no longer causing problems. After reclaiming the RT, I rode from there to Jacksonville, Florida, for the annual Iron Butt Association Pizza Party. Heading back to the west coast anyway, I opted to attempt a 50CC, a coast-to-coast IBA certified ride from there to Coronado, California, in less than fifty hours, which I successfully completed before finally riding north to Folsom and home.

It was time to listen to my body's protests demanding attention. Hanging up my multi-day rallying hat, I focused my limited energies on speaking engagements and conferences, and restricted rallying to a few twenty-four hour events closer to home.

2006

Four endemic countries remain: Afghanistan, India, Nigeria, and Pakistan. Outbreaks in Yemen and Indonesia—which suffer the largest, single-country outbreaks in recent years— are successfully stopped.

2008

Polio eradication becomes the World Health Organization's "top operational priority."

CHAPTER 22

Sitting out the 2007 Iron Butt Rally challenged my resolve to quit entering multi-day events. Despite my better judgment, I found myself once more getting ready to ride in the 2009 event. I shipped my bike to BMW Atlanta rather than ride across the country to the start, then took it out for a short test ride to ensure it had made the trip without incident.

"I'd recommend replacing the one on the rear and the one on the sidecar," Bob Woldridge, the dealer, was pretty forceful in his assessment of my tires. "I don't think you'll finish the Rally with those."

"I beg to differ, Bob," I was equally adamant in my opinion. "They've got plenty of mileage on them." Disagreeing with his conclusions, I paid for the service and gathered my gear.

"Your bike, your choice," he concluded as I got on the RT. "Have a safe ride in any case."

I felt confident in my decision as I rode the final two hundred miles to Spartanburg, South Carolina, and parked it alongside the other bikes in the hotel. I was glad I had two navigation units in case one failed since all the bonus locations would only be available as GPS coordinates, whereas in past events, written directions for bonuses were included in the rally paperwork. As I finished the final touches, I noticed how, with the exception of the sidecar, my bike now looked like the others with auxiliary lights, a fuel cell and a custom seat, made specifically for me by Rick Mayer to accommodate the scoliosis in my spine.

Retiring to my room after the opening banquet, I opened my rally pack to begin planning the first leg. *Ah, what the hell, may as well go to Key West,* I thought, opting to skip the more obvious choice of Dike Bridge on Chappaquiddick Island with its much higher points but higher challenges of a ferry crossing coupled with a presidential visit.

Instead, I drove south into an impending storm. Key West is included in almost every Iron Butt Rally, and is usually considered a sucker bonus; one only a fool would attempt given the long distance, two lane road, and low speed limits. Unfortunately, routing has never been my strong suit.

The rain quickly destroyed my 'nearly waterproof' GPS, and my back-up unit failed soon after. Huddled under an overpass, I tried fixing them, wrapping the soaked one in a Ziploc bag. It worked intermittently for the next two hundred miles before quitting for good.

I pulled into the Miccosukee Resort and Casino in Miami near midnight, and had to wait until an hour before sunrise to take the daylight-only photo of a dock next to the pond behind the hotel. I decided to take a rest bonus, during which time I actually earned points for not riding and wasn't allowed to collect bonuses. I thought I'd check into the resort for a decent couple hours of sleep rather than my usual spot on a picnic table, but with the cheapest room costing $160, I balked.

"I don't want to buy the damn bed, I just want a place to put my head down for a few hours!"

The clerk realized he wasn't going to sell me a room, so he offered a more creative solution. "If you join our player's club, the room is only $29," he whispered.

"What's the catch? How much does it cost to join the club?" I assumed there had to be a trick somewhere.

"Nothing. We just want people to come here and gamble, but if we can get them to pay full price for the room as well, we win all the way around," he confessed.

"Sign me up." Always willing to accept a reasonable deal, I grabbed the key, went to my room, and set my alarm for two short hours of sleep.

The theme of the Rally was 'Scene of the Crime,' with each bonus having a connection to some notorious illegal event: historical, recent, stupid, or humorous. The crime at the resort was described as follows:

Police responded to a call that two men were breaking into cars in the hotel's parking lot. Upon arrival they captured one suspect but another escaped, and despite signs warning of the presence of alligators, jumped into a retaining pond. He began to swim away, but was swiftly dragged under water and killed by one of the pond's reptiles.

Wandering around the hotel, I noticed a 'Do Not Feed the Alligators' sign and assumed I was in the correct location. I took a photo and went back to the bike to check my paperwork before taking off.

For the first time, each bonus requiring a photo included a sample of the picture, and as I compared them, I realized I had made a mistake. I returned to the back of the hotel and the pond, and circled the water until I found the correct sign, 'Danger Live Alligators' at the end of a different wooden dock.

Stepping onto the pier to get the photo, my crutches slipped out from under me. I fell to the ground and skidded along the splintered surface, unable to stop as I careened toward the water.

"No! Not in the water!" I screamed, although no one could hear me. Because I held onto my crutches to keep them from flying into the pond, I had no way to grab onto the wet boards, so I kept sliding closer to the end of the dock. With one arm dangling over the edge I finally came to a halt, my camera strap still attached to my wrist. My crutches flew out over the water, but thankfully, I was able to hang onto them, pulling them back next to me as I lay on my back, catching my breath.

I turned my head in time to see my flag, which I had lost sometime during my tumble, slowly sink under the murky surface. Using one of my crutches as a fishing pole, I pulled it back to dry land, wrung it out, and slowly got back on my feet.

"Well, that wasn't much fun," I said aloud. "Let's not try that again." I made my way very carefully up the ramp, stopped to take the correct photo, and left before any of the alligators discovered me.

~

"Skert, I need a GPS. Both of mine have gone belly up. Do you think you can help me find one?" I'd called Carol Youorski, or Skert as she's known in the long-distance riding community. "There's no way I can figure out where to go without one."

"Meet me at the Atlanta BMW dealer; I'll bring mine. You can get it back to me after the Rally." When I pulled into the dealer, she came out and greeted me with, "I've got the GPS but I forgot the power cord. I'm going to run over to Target to see if I can find a replacement." I took advantage of the break to take a short nap.

"This is the only one I could find that might work. It's for a car, but let's try it." I wasn't optimistic. We both fiddled with it, but it turned out to be useless on my bike.

"I can loan you my Zumo." Bob, the BMW dealer, had just shown up, and hearing of my dilemma, offered the GPS from his personal bike. He called his wife, who deftly disconnected it and brought it to the shop.

"This will work great. Thanks Bob. I'll ship it back after the Rally." Finally I had a working unit, and headed for St. Charles, Illinois, and the first checkpoint.

By the time I reached the hotel the Zumo had quit, a victim of poor wiring. *Are you kidding me?* I had now gone through five GPS units, one less than the number of bonuses I had managed to visit.

Paul Glaves, the friend who had fixed the broken clutch after the 2005 IBR, saw me swearing at my bike and came over. "What's going on, Bob?"

"This damn GPS isn't working; every one I touch seems to break. I need to get into scoring and get some rest before the next leg bonuses come out!" I yelled before I could catch myself. Calming down, I continued, "I have to get this one to work or I'm finished."

"Let me take a look at it," he suggested.

"I need to go in and stop the clock to confirm I was here before the checkpoint closes. Once I do that I'll come back out and we can get at it." Within minutes of my return he had the bike apart, fixed the faulty wiring, and had the GPS working perfectly. I went back inside to get ready for scoring, and, once finished, went up to my room, drained. I passed out on the bed in my full gear.

Just before 4 a.m. I awoke to pick up the Leg Two Rally pack. I took back to my room to plan a route. Three high point, timed bonuses had to be visited before 5 p.m. that day, so I took off, deciding to plan the rest of my route later. I raced first to the Frank Lloyd Wright Visitor Center in Wisconsin, then to the Hobo Museum in Britt, Iowa, and grabbed a quick photo of the Surf Ballroom in Clear Lake on my way to the final timed bonus, a covered bridge in Winterset, Iowa.

As I pulled into the gravel parking lot a sharp rock punctured the tire on the sidecar. This was becoming downright comical! I felt like laughing. *What else can go wrong?*

In the middle of nowhere, I had to hastily piece together a solution since I didn't carry a spare. Taking all the gear out of the sidecar and tying it to the passenger seat on the bike to lighten the weight, I rode another three hours before noticing a Michelin dealer in what looked like a farmhouse.

I'm not sure he knew what to make of me standing in his doorway. "I'm sorry to disturb you, but I was wondering if you have a tire that might fit my sidecar? I don't have time to wait until morning." I briefly explained the necessity to keep moving.

"Let's see if I have something you can use." Despite the late hour, he was willing to help. "I've got this Yamaha motorcycle front tire. I don't know if it'll work." Pulling it down from the wire racks in his shop, we set it on the floor and went to work removing the damaged tire from its rim, tossing it into the corner.

"Here goes," we both struggled to get the new, stiffer tire onto the rim. Amazingly, it worked. I knew it was only a temporary fix, but hoped it would at least get me to the next checkpoint in California. I paid the man, thanked him profusely, hopped back on the bike, and kept riding.

At the Barbed Wire Museum bonus in La Crosse, Kansas, I spent a few minutes commiserating with George Barnes, the winner of my first Iron Butt Rally in 1999, about the frustrations of a rally where paper maps were useless. "I am not at all impressed with this high tech rallying," he moaned. "I'm an old-fashioned guy. I like having things written out, and I like seeing where I'm going."

"You're not going to get any argument from me on that one. I hate not being able to have the backup of paper when things go wrong," I agreed. Unfortunately, on this rally I was speaking from experience. I continued on to Washington, picking up another four bonuses before noticing my rear tire was down to the wear bars.

"Damn it, you were right." I was on the phone with Bob, the BMW dealer in Atlanta. "I'm going to need a rear and sidecar tire to finish this Rally." Bob routed me to a dealership in Oregon, some four hundred miles away, but much closer to the checkpoint than returning to his shop.

Three hundred and fifty miles later I arrived and handed the mechanic the keys. The Rally rules had changed; the rider now had to be with his bike at all times when it was being repaired. The rules said nothing about being awake, or who had to perform the work. "I brought you a cot. Set it up here next to the bike and get some sleep." The mechanic got no argument from me. I slept soundly while he finished.

Needing to make up the seven hundred mile detour, I hustled toward Santa Ana, California, and the second checkpoint. I gave up on the idea of picking up any bonuses along the way, just wanting to make it before the time window closed and I'd be disqualified.

And though I was used to summer heat in Folsom, the 118 degree temperatures in the Mojave Desert caused havoc with the fuel lines on the bike. I assumed vapor lock was preventing the gas from getting to the engine, and since I knew I had fuel in the auxiliary tank, I stopped beneath an overpass to fix the problem and give the bike a rest. Sweating profusely in my full riding gear, I stripped down to my shorts and poured water over my body.

Cars slowed down to see if I needed assistance before taking one look at me and racing away from what surely looked to them like a lunatic. Pulling the fuel filter off, I noticed an air bubble in the line. After cleaning it, I put it back together, reinstalled it on the bike, and took off for the hotel.

"BAM!" The noise startled me just as the bike jerked suddenly to the right.

What the hell is going on? I fought to maintain control and keep the bike in a straight line, recognizing the all too familiar feeling of dread. *It's the sidecar: either the tire or the axle.* I avoided grabbing the brakes and causing a further loss of control, and instead, eased off the gas, allowing the RT to slow down on its own.

A car behind me put on its flashers, providing protection as I guided the bike to the shoulder of the busy interstate, where I removed my helmet, and got off the bike to see what had happened.

The tire had exploded. I couldn't believe it. I'd just had it replaced. Sighing, I pulled out my cell phone, and called a tow company.

"We can be there in about two hours. Our minimum charge for towing a vehicle like yours will be $1200." I hung up and dialed my wife who was already waiting to meet me at the checkpoint.

"Patti, I need help. Do you have any ideas?" Within minutes, she called me back.

"Reiner and Lisa Kappenberger are here, and Reiner says he has a jack you can use. We'll put it in the car and come to you. I have your spare with me; we can put it on when we get there. Give me your exact location." Even though I'd changed tires in Atlanta, Patti had already packed the spare so we didn't need to find one on short notice. I was only a few miles from the hotel and if they hurried, I could still make the checkpoint in time. I waited impatiently alongside the speeding cars on the freeway, a bit worried when I saw lights flashing and a Highway Patrol officer pull in behind me.

"I'll just hang out here with you until they arrive. Safer if I have my lights on so folks don't hit you." Her presence helped distract me until my crew arrived, and after changing the tire, I rode the final miles into the checkpoint just before the penalty window opened.

Leg Three started out promising. Planning a good route to qualify as a finisher despite the challenges of the previous leg, I picked up several bonuses in Nevada and Utah on my way to Oregon. I took a photo of a horse farm near Corvallis and grabbed a quick bite to eat as the sun set in the western sky. I'd already stopped to replace yet another rear tire, and was getting frustrated with the frequency of repairs I'd had to make. I knew the added weight of the sidecar wears tires out far more frequently than on a traditional two-wheeled motorcycle, but this was getting to be absurd. Figuring I was now safe to make it to the finish before needing any more work, I headed east on Highway 126, crossing through the mountains in Oregon.

As I cruised down the eastern slopes, mesmerized by the beauty of stars overhead and the solitude of the road, I felt the bike moving in an entirely new way; it was leaning like a traditional two-wheeled motorcycle, not a two-wheeled motorcycle with a leaner.

"What NOW?" I yelled inside my helmet, incredulous that another part had obviously broken.

Normally I manually activated the mechanism that allowed the sidecar to lean when I rode through curves, but it had somehow come loose and the bike was leaning on its own. I'd never experienced the normal movement of a motorcycle, but drew from conversations I'd overheard about putting pressure on the handlebar closest to the direction of the turn. I tried slowing down to keep the bike under control, the tight curves and steep downhill demanding my full attention.

For a brief moment I was actually enjoying the sweeping motion of the bike on the turns when I heard the leaner jam between the sidecar and the bike, removing whatever chance of control that remained. The sidecar was now pushing the bike to the left, and I could no longer make a right turn. Knowing the crash was inevitable, I applied the brakes carefully, hoping for the best.

As I skidded to a stop, the bike rolled, landed on top of me, and pinned my legs in the dirt. With blood dripping down my face, I yanked off my helmet, only to watch it bounce down the hillside when I placed it on the ground. I reached up to hit the kill switch and silence the engine, and assessed my situation.

Great. Out in the middle of nowhere, can't move, can't get to my cell phone even if there's coverage this far from civilization. Nothing feels broken, but if someone doesn't come along soon, I may freeze in place. I want someone to drive by, but I definitely don't want anyone to hit me. Lying on the wrong side of the road, the sidecar sticking out onto the pavement, I put my head down in the dirt. There was nothing I could do but wait.

I heard the distinctive sound of a diesel engine before the headlights came into view. I reached up to the bike, turned the key in the ignition, and hoped the RT's lights would alert the driver to my situation. Realizing I was hearing not one, but two trucks—and they were approaching from opposite directions—I hoped they'd see me before they hit me.

Remarkably, two women, each pulling horse trailers, slowed and stopped, jumping out of their trucks to see if I was alive.

"Help me get this off of me, and hand me my crutches," I implored, relieving them of any anxiety that I was badly injured.

"And if one of you could find my helmet I'd really appreciate it. I think it's somewhere down off the edge a bit over there." I pointed down the road where I'd heard it crunching on the gravel as it rolled.

"Found it! Didn't make it too far before hitting a boulder. Lucky for you it did, or it might have ended up at the bottom of that ravine." Given my circumstances, I was happy for any luck at the moment.

"My cell phone works out here. I'll call someone to come out. Shouldn't be a problem," one of the women reassured me. I silently gave thanks for having the foresight to sign up for a towing service before the start of the Rally.

A young man in a Ford Explorer camper conversion stopped to give us all freshly made coffee while we waited for help to arrive. For a few moments it almost felt like a party, the four of us sitting alongside the road, drinking fresh coffee and sharing stories.

When the tow truck arrived, the driver instructed, "I'll need you to sit on the bike and hold the sidecar while the cable pulls it onto the tilt bed of the truck." While he secured everything in place with straps, I thanked everyone for their kindness and climbed into the passenger seat for the ride into town. As we rode together down the mountainside, I told the story of the Iron Butt Rally, PolioPlus, and Rotary.

"Well, bud, today is your lucky day. As it turns out, you don't need a motorcycle repair shop, you need a welder to fix your sidecar. I just happen to fabricate race cars, and if you're okay with it, I'd like to take this rig to my shop and see what I can do for you." I stared at him.

"I need to get some rest, I'll need a place to sleep," I mumbled, reality setting in. I still had to follow the rules of the Rally; I had to be physically present while any work was done.

""I've got a couch in the office; you can sleep there while I assess the damages," he assured me.

He spent the next seven hours completely removing the sidecar, re-welding the brackets and leaner and re-assembling the rig. It was one of the cleanest, nicest welding jobs I had ever seen.

"What do I owe you? Can you accept a credit card?" I wanted to settle the bill before heading out and attempting to reach Spokane before I was time barred.

"I looked you up last night on the Internet while you were asleep and found your website. I'm impressed with what Rotary is trying to accomplish and what you've been doing to help. You don't owe me a thing. Consider it my contribution."

"Well, I certainly appreciate your generosity. It means a lot." Grateful for his help, I thanked him profusely. My only regret is that I never learned his name.

I knew I had just enough time to get to the finish if I skipped any further bonus collecting. In the first leg of the Rally some of my photos had been disqualified, the size of the pictures not meeting the exacting requirements of the scoring rules. Somehow my camera had been set in such a way that it randomly changed sizing, some photos complying with the rules, others too large. In addition, some pictures I knew I had taken mysteriously disappeared from my files when they were downloaded at scoring. If I could somehow find the missing pictures, perhaps I'd still have enough points to be considered a finisher.

I got to the hotel in time, and ran to my room to get ready for scoring, but was unable to locate the missing photos. I realized that even if I had it would have been too late to claim them since scoring for the previous legs had already closed. Happy, at least, to have made it safely to Spokane after a torturous rally, I was nonetheless disappointed to record my first DNF (did not finish) because of an inadequate point total.

2009

The new bivalent oral poliovirus vaccine is used for the first time in Afghanistan. This two-strain vaccine was found to produce a significantly higher immune response in clinical trials than either the single or triple-strain versions.

CHAPTER 23

"What do you think about us putting on a ride to eat?" Patti stood in the kitchen finishing up the dishes from dinner.

We'd been discussing alternative ways to raise money for PolioPlus over our evening meal.

"If riders are crazy enough to go to Pink's in Los Angeles to meet their friends for a hot dog at midnight, they'd probably be willing to come to Folsom for a luncheon. Heck, I've been crazy enough to ride to Pink's myself, only to turn around and ride back home the same night."

Long-distance riders are an odd bunch, often travelling across the country for a lunch gathering, only to hop back on the bike and return home after the tire kicking and swapping of stories are over. The entire United States is their backyard, and most Iron Butt members are usually looking for any excuse to go for a ride.

If I could turn a Ride to Eat into a PolioPlus event, I'd be able to continue raising awareness for our campaign while spending the day with my riding friends.

"We can combine a meal with a talk, and if we give out the Paul Harris Fellowship Award we'll be able to publically honor the recipients. Let me email Mike Kneebone and see if he's willing to be our first speaker."

Always a draw in the Iron Butt community, Mike's attendance would create more interest in an inaugural event. Inviting fellow long-distance enthusiasts to come to Folsom, our plan was to host a banquet luncheon honoring those who have contributed to PolioPlus along with an opportunity to visit with friends and share motorcycling stories.

Mike readily agreed, and once we had lined up the president of the Iron Butt Association as a guest speaker, we put the word out on several riding listservs, inviting IBA members and non-members alike.

For our first Paul Harris Fellowship ceremony, we handed out awards to Jeff Earls, Tom Melchild, Tom Loftus, and Joe Zulaski for their efforts on behalf of PolioPlus. Their work has helped keep attention on the goals of Rotary in the motorcycling community.

Our first Ride to Eat was a great success, and without much discussion we decided to turn it into an annual event. Dubbing it the 'NoPolio!Rally,' we expanded the luncheon the following year to include an eight-hour ride.

Our first route designers, Reiner and Lisa Kappenberger, created an event that was fun for both new and experienced rallyists, inviting them to experience some of our favorite local roads.

The NoPolio! Motorcycle Rally with our current Routemaster, Alan Pratt, consists of a Friday night barbeque, a twelve-hour mini rally during the day on Saturday, followed by a finisher's banquet in the evening.

Seeing riders from all over the country express their support for the fight to eradicate polio has been as heartwarming as the welcomes I received for my many solo rides. Their generous checks to the local Rotary chapter inspires me to keep going despite my own aches and pains. Watching them ride off with bright yellow stickers on their bikes reassures me the word will continue to spread.

2012

The worldwide total of polio cases has decreased to fewer than 223 cases. India has passed the one-year mark since their last reported polio case and has been declared polio free.

2013

Civil war in Syria leads to disruption in public health delivery services. Previously eradicated, polio re-emerges as at least ten cases of paralysis are confirmed. Experts believe the source of the virus was Pakistan.

EPILOGUE

What previously took me only ten minutes to accomplish now takes thirty. Waking up, getting out of bed, getting dressed, and heading into the kitchen for breakfast is an hour-long task. A master at finding workarounds for any problem I might encounter, I realize how much I have been accommodating my increasing fatigue and decreasing mobility. Pain, always a part of my experience, now demands more of my attention. The shaking from palsy in my right hand is beginning to interfere with my fine motor control. Thankfully, riding has not been affected. Once on the bike, with my full focus on the road, I still find the freedom that I experienced on my first ride at thirteen.

Having just celebrated my sixty-sixth birthday, I feel the years. My parents, still alive, remind me of the longevity in my family tree, but the wear and tear from the polio and its complications make each day a bit harder and I wonder if my life will have a shorter trajectory. When the 2013 Iron Butt Rally came within miles of my home, I longed to join them, but know my multi-day rallies really are over. Instead, I sat with a group of friends and cheered as riders raced into the hotel to stop the clock at the checkpoint. In the meantime, I participate in single-day rallying and ride as often as my schedule allows. I still intend to come skidding in at the finish, no matter when that time may be.

It's been thirty years since I sat in the doctor's office and listened to his predictions for my future. While he was correct about the diagnosis of Post Polio syndrome, fortunately he was wrong about me. Whether I have simply been too stubborn or too lucky, I have yet to succumb to a wheelchair. Deciding to return to motorcycling may have saved my life. I know it saved my sanity and has given me a deeper sense of purpose.

Likewise, I have no intention of giving up the fight to eradicate polio worldwide. If someone had told me forty years ago where my life would end up, I would have laughed at him. I didn't believe I really had much to offer other than paying my Rotary club dues and contributing a bit of money now and then to a cause. Now I understand in my heart what Horace Mann meant when he penned the words, "Be ashamed to die until you have won some victory for humanity." If I can follow that advice, my life will have been a success. In 2000, during my first visit to Africa, I made a promise to the children of the world as well as to myself that I would continue to ride my motorcycle and speak whenever possible about this awesome project taken on by Rotary and our partners: the Bill and Melinda Gates Foundation; WHO, UNICEF and CDC. There are many diseases and problems, but few that are within our grasp to conquer, and at such a small cost.

I can also say with absolute truthfulness that, in looking back, I have gotten far more out of life than I can ever give back. Living in America, I enjoy the comforts that we all take for granted: clean water; more clothes than I will ever need; whatever food I desire; electricity to operate my gadgets and tools; too many motorcycles and cars; an occupation that pays well; immediate medical treatment; the list goes on. I am indeed blessed.

It is because of all the people who have supported my passion that any degree of personal success has been achieved. I am rich with friends who continually demonstrate their willingness to assist whenever I need a hand. People I may have just met astound me with their offers to help me navigate my way out of any difficulties I may be facing. I have been given food, fuel, mechanical repairs, transportation, medical treatment, housing, and most importantly, friendships wherever I go. Strangers approach me when I'm on the road, strike up conversations about the stickers on the sidecar, and after learning about Rotary, reach into their pockets and hand me money to forward to PolioPlus. Chief Sitting Bull said, "Let us put our minds together and see what life we can make for our children." That has been the wisdom of PolioPlus and the partnerships that are accomplishing the total eradication of a virus that, a mere sixty years ago, was the most feared disease in America.

Polio, for the most part, is silent. Most victims show few—or no—symptoms, thus allowing it to spread rapidly before it is noticed. For every paralytic case, it is presumed there are hundreds of unknown carriers. One unidentified carrier can bring the disease to an unsuspecting population, including into the developed world where there are pockets of anti-vaccination protesters. Without quick action, the virus can once again spread. In 2005, outbreaks occurred both in an Amish community in Minnesota and in Indonesia, the world's fourth most populous country. They were stopped with a rapid response public health vaccination program. We are seeing the growing resurgence of diseases, such as measles and whooping cough, which were once rare but are returning as parents refuse to vaccinate their children. A recent outbreak of a polio-like illness in California, paralyzing limbs overnight, is a scary reminder that these diseases cause genuine damage. For many viruses there are no cures but we do have means of prevention, and for polio in particular, time is of the essence.

The fight continues. Three countries, Nigeria, Pakistan, and Afghanistan, have yet to fully immunize their populations. The challenges are many. Anti-vaccination efforts often based on false or misleading stories open the possibility of a resurgence of polio in the developed world. Workers have been assassinated as anti-

American sentiment flames fears among rural villages that the vaccines are part of a plot to sterilize babies. The Taliban have blocked all vaccinations in the Swat Valley of Pakistan, leading to an increase in polio cases. Outbreaks have occurred in Angola, Chad, the Democratic Republic of Congo, Sudan, Nepal, Kazakhstan, Tajikistan, Turkmenistan, and Russia. War in Syria has disrupted their previously highly efficient public health system, resulting in a sharp upturn in new cases of polio, the origins of which have been traced to Pakistan. The United Nations, authorized to operate only through sovereign states, has been stymied in its efforts to get the vaccine to the rebel populations since all efforts must be coordinated with Damascus. As of this writing, the Syrian government has blocked all attempts to create a delivery route through Turkey.

The vaccine must be kept cold at all times, which is difficult, as it is transported to remote areas with no electricity. Changing weather conditions, which often wash out dirt roads, keep workers from reaching children. Anger at local governments for their lack of attention to sanitation and reliable, clean water supplies provokes resistance to the push to vaccinate: "Why should we take this when you are failing us and our children are dying of fever or diarrhea?" Community health efforts must cover all areas, not just polio. Building trust requires person-to-person contact, creating an environment where mothers and fathers believe their concerns are being heard.

Locating and immunizing remote, nomadic populations has been a major effort in Nigeria where the National Stop Transmission of Polio program, supported by the Nigerian government, has begun tracking hard-to-reach populations. Such nomadic groups are often strongholds of the disease, and may carry the virus with them to unsuspecting villagers when they come to markets to trade their goods. Previous efforts in the successful fight to eradicate smallpox worldwide found a similar problem, as these remote populations were where the last vestiges of the disease were located.

Progress is being made. India, long thought to be one of the most challenging populations to immunize because its high density and poor sanitation created the ideal environment for the spread of the virus, celebrated its third year without a case of polio and was certified polio-free in March 2014, along with ten other countries in Southeast Asia. Despite war and deep anti-American sentiment, Afghanistan and Pakistan have seen significant reductions in the past two years. The concerted efforts to reach nomadic populations appear to be having results as fewer cases of polio were reported in Nigeria between 2012 and 2013.

"There are worse diseases than polio that demand our attention."

"More efforts should be paid to sanitation and other public health issues."

"Wars are thwarting efforts to bring vaccines to rebels in Syria."

"We should opt for control rather than eradication of polio, and put our efforts toward other epidemics."

I've heard all the arguments that polio immunization efforts are no longer warranted, that the enthusiasm for such programs is waning, and that we should settle for controlling outbreaks rather than full eradication. However, what has been learned in this fight can be applied to other causes and other diseases, potentially helping to end needless suffering, especially in children. Everyone benefits from the knowledge we have gained in how to find and connect with people to gain their trust and help improve their lives.

We are close to winning this war, but not without continued efforts, attention, and money. Vaccinations are easy to administer, cheap to produce, and highly effective. While many diseases deserve our attention, few are as inexpensive to prevent as polio.

Experts suggest eradicating polio will save billions in long-term costs, and it would be a shame to waste the money that has already been spent to come as far as we have.

The 1952 epidemic in the United States was the worst in our history, and within three years cases were reduced to a negligible number with the simple administration of a shot in the arm. Had that shot been available only a few years earlier my life may have taken a dramatically different course. Witnessing the effects of immunization firsthand—both at home and in Africa—ensuring every last child in the world is vaccinated is my personal goal. PolioPlus, leading the way, needs your support to finish this fight. I remain steadfastly committed to preventing unnecessary suffering when something so inexpensive and easy to administer is available. My hope is to still be alive when we are able to celebrate the end of this dread disease. I would love to devote my remaining years to other equally urgent needs, most specifically providing wheelchairs for those who have been affected by polio, and promoting literacy worldwide. Hopefully, I will continue to be a rebel with a cause for many years to come, but that the cause will no longer be polio.

2014

The World Health Organization certifies
the entire South-East Asia region polio-free
as India celebrates three years without a new case.

BIBLIOGRAPHY AND REFERENCES

Efforts to Eradicate Polio Worldwide:

Aleccia, JoNel. "Syrian outbreak could spread to Europe, experts warn," NBC News (Nov. 7, 2013)

Amos, Deborah. "As Polio Spreads in Syria, Politics Thwarts Vaccination Efforts," NPR.org (December 3, 2013)

Callaway, Ewan. "Public Health: Polio's moving target" *Nature International Weekly Journal of Science*, Volume 496 Issue 7445 (April 17, 2013)

Chan, Dr. Margaret. "WHO Director-General Celebrates Polio-Free India," (February 11, 2014)

Doughton, Sandi. "Endgame for polio? Gates touting new plan to wipe it out," *Seattle Times*, (April 24, 2013)

The Final Inch, Vermillion Films, Irene Taylor Brodsky, Producer

Gladstone, Rick. "Syria polio scare; UN to vaccinate 2.5 million," *Seattle Times*, (October 26, 2013)

Kluger, Jeffrey. "Polio and Politics. A great scourge might soon be gone, but war, mistrust and even the death of Osama Bin Laden could get in the way," *Time*, (January 14, 2013)

McNeil, Jr., Donald G. "Gates Calls for a Final Push to

Eradicate Polio," *The New York Times*, (January 31, 2011)

"Our Progress Against Polio," Centers for Disease Control and Prevention, http://www.cdc.gov/polio/progress/

Franklin D Roosevelt and Polio:

<http://en.wikipedia.org/wiki/Franklin_D._Roosevelt>

Kehret, Peg, *Small Steps: The Year I Got Polio*, (Albert Whitman & Co., 1996)

Iron Butt Association and Iron Butt Rally:

www.ironbutt.org

March of Dimes and polio:

<http://www.marchofdimes.com>

<http://en.wikipedia.org/wiki/March_of_Dimes>

Polio, the Disease and History:

A Paralyzing Fear: The Story of Polio in America. PBS, Nina Gilden Seavey and Paul Wagner, Producers, 2004

Bloom, Stuart, and Ingrid Geesink. "Essay on Science and Society: A Brief History of Polio Vaccines," *Science Magazine*, Vol. 288 no. 5471 (2 June 2000)

"History of Polio," Polio Global Eradication Initiative, <http://www.polioeradication.org/Polioandprevention/Historyof polio.aspx>

"Hilary Koprowski," <http://en.wikipedia.org/wiki/Hilary_Koprowski>

Palka, Joe. "Salk Polio Vaccine Conquered Terrifying Disease," NPR, (April 12, 2005)

"Poliomyelitis (infantile paralysis, polio)" NY State Department of Health

<http://www.health.ny.gov/diseases/communicable/poliomyelitis/fact_sheet (January 2012)

<http://en.wikipedia.org/wiki/Poliomyelitis>

<http://polioforever.wordpress.com/polio-timeline>

<http://en.wikipedia.org/wiki/Poliovirus>

Rutty, Christopher J., PhD., "The History of Polio Content," Health Heritage Research Services

"Albert Sabin," <http://en.wikipedia.org/wiki/Albert_Sabin>

"Jonas Salk," <http://en.wikipedia.org/wiki/Jonas_Salk>

"The History of Polio; A Hypertext Timeline," <http://www.eds-resources.com/poliotimeline.htm>

The Polio Crusade, American Experience, WGBH/PBS, Sarah Colt Producer, 2009

"Whatever Happened to Polio," Smithsonian Museum of American History <http://amhistory.si.edu/polio/>

Post Polio Syndrome:

"Post-Polio Fact Sheet," National Institute of Neurological Disorders and Stroke, <http://www.ninds.nih.gov/disorders/post_polio/detail_post_polio.htm>

Post-Polio Health International, <http://www.post-polio.org/>

<http://en.wikipedia.org/wiki/Post-polio_syndrome>

Rotary International:

<http://www.rotary.org>

ACKNOWLEDGMENTS

After fifteen years of attempts it finally sunk in that I am not a writer. Had Lynda Lahman not agreed to write this book, it would still be locked somewhere in my mind. Thank you, Lynda, for tackling a two-year task where all the proceeds go to charity.

I would also like to express my sincere appreciation to the following people who have been responsible for my being able to continue my quest for total world eradication of polio:

Brian Buckley, for his continued monetary assistance for my rides and for paying the editing costs of publishing this book. My parents, who have given me a lifetime of support and 'tuff' love. My wife, Patti, for supporting everything on my bucket list regardless of the difficulty. A&S Motorsports for the donation of two BMW motorcycles and thousands of dollars in service. The California Highway Patrol, whose commissioners have been the honorary chairs of my PolioPlus Motorcycle Rides since 1998. Rick Mayer Custom Saddles. My webmaster, Jon Greene.

Cliff Dochterman, my Rotary mentor. Neil Cook, my attorney, who has given me two decades of humor and numerous reasons to quit riding along with an equal number to continue. Tony Hennessy, my Aussie riding sidekick. Mario Winkelman of LDComfort Riding Gear. Hannigan Sidecars donation of a custom sidecar for my motorcycle in 1999. Mike Kneebone, for allowing me to compete in three Iron Butt Rallies. Steve Chalmers, for letting me compete in his MERA events. Tom Melchild, for making the CAL 24 a fundraiser for PolioPlus. The Rotary Club of Folsom, for financing the startup costs of the NoPolio! Motorcycle Rally, a fundraiser for PolioPlus. Ken Meese and Ernie Azevedo, for countless hours creating a way to run a car tire on my motorcycle and for being there whenever assistance was needed. Bill McKenna and Reiner and Lisa Kappenberger, the original rallymasters of the NoPolio! Motorcycle Rally. Allan Pratt, the rallymaster of the last three NoPolio! Motorcycle Rallies. Miller BMW, BMW of Little Rock, BMW Motorcycles of Atlanta, Irv Seaver Motorcycles, and South Sound BMW have donated labor and/or parts to keep me on the road. Nolan Helmets, CALSCI Inc, Michelin Tires, and MotoLights have donated top of the line equipment to the PolioPlus motorcycle rides.

The entire long-distance motorcycle riding community, including but not limited to: Bill Thweat, Brian Boberick, Dale Wilson, Lisa Landry, Jeff Earls, Jim Owen, Pat Widder, Jerry White, Dave Biasotti, Tom Loftus, Karen Bolin, Bob Higdon, Carol Youorski, John Chaney, Ron Smith, Bob St. George, Jason Jonas, John Ryan, Joe Zulaski, Paul and Voni Glaves, and countless others.

Tom Almassy, Rally shirt specialist, Irv Dickson Machinery. Eldorado Physical Therapy. My doctors, who have kept me physically able to continue the quest: Dr. Rob DeBruin, Dr. Guy Guilfoy, and Dr. Henry Sundermier. The world membership of Rotary International, for being so supportive of my endeavors. And hundreds of others who are not mentioned because of space and fading memory.

Believe me when I say, "On behalf of the children of the world, thank you."

~ Bob Mutchler

Without Bob there would be no story. I appreciate your willingness to answer difficult questions and dig deeper into memories you may have preferred to keep buried. Thanks to Patti Mutchler for your support and endless supply of food during the long hours of interviews. I am grateful for the chance to have met Bob's parents, Alice and Bob Mutchler, which added depth to Bob's early years. Tobie Stevens, as always, your excellent eye and the gift of your time brought the photographs to life. Jami Carpenter, who would have thought all those years ago that sitting in front of you in Mr. Willingham's torturously boring US History class would result in this collaboration. Thank you for your gentle guidance in helping shape the story with the right words. Tom Melchild, thanks for sharing your stories of the Cal 24 and its involvement with PolioPlus. Suzanne Campbell, I greatly appreciate you turning the vision in my head into the reality of the cover for the book. Helen Towers, Jackie Swanson, and Dick Ryon: your willingness to be candid helped in so many ways; thanks for taking the time to provide such honest feedback. And to my husband, Terry, who listened to my ideas and inspired their development through questions and comments, and spent days with me on the road back and forth to California interviewing Bob; you are my greatest fan and my best friend. Thank you for everything.

~ Lynda Lahman

ABOUT THE AUTHOR

A mental skills coach for athletes with a background of over thirty years as a psychotherapist, Lynda Lahman brings a unique perspective to the world of long-distance motorcycle riding. She and her husband, Terry, have competed in two Iron Butt Rallies and numerous other endurance events.

Lynda is the author of *Two-Up: Navigating a Relationship 1,000 Miles at a Time*, and writes a regular column, "Perspective," for the *Iron Butt Magazine*.

As a result of her work on this book, Lynda has become an active member of Rotary International.

31310928R00158

Made in the USA
Charleston, SC
13 July 2014